MacCallum &

	1862								
May	1	257	By	Building Yard					✓
June	"	266	"	do					✓
July	"	273	"	do					✓
Augt	"	280	"	do			4	2	✓
Sept	"	285	"	do		07	15	7	✓
Oct	"	292	"	do		987	8	1	✓
Nov	1863	299	"	do		2484	18	2	✓
Jany	"	314	"	do		1118	15	4	✓
Feby	"	321	"	do		2524	18	7	✓
March	4	329	"	Cash		1220	"	"	
April	1	338	"	Building Yard		7501	2	8	✓
May	"	345	"	do		684	13	7	✓
May	"	346	"	do		1359	19	10	✓
June	"	354	"	do		883	1	10	✓
						28574	8	10	
July	1	363	By	Building Yard		716	11	"	✓
"	"	368	"	do		245	14	4	✓
						962	5	4	
Augt	1	372	By	Building Yard		812	4	"	✓
Sept	26	376	"	Cash		4	"	"	✓
"	"	379	"	Building Yard		707	"	7	✓
"	"	382	"	Discount		6	18	"	✓
						1604	"	2	
	1863								
Decr	1	402	By	Building Yard		253	8	11	✓
						253	8	11	
	1864								
Jany	1	412	By	Building Yard		1043	5	"	✓
Feby	"	419	"	do		900	1	"	✓
						1943	6		

BED OF NAILS

To Keith
With good wishes
[signature]
14·3·97

Front cover: PS Loch Lomond with Captain James Lang on the bridge circa. 1840

Dedication

To: PM and PB

A Bed of Nails

The history of P MacCallum & Sons Ltd of
Greenock 1781–1981
a study in survival

The Mid Harbour, Greenock in about 1890

John R Hume and Michael S Moss
Lang & Fulton, Greenock

A Bed of Nails

The history of P MacCallum & Sons Ltd of Greenock,
1781–1981 – a study in survival

British Library Cataloguing in Production Data
Hume, John Robert
MacCallum
1. Bed of Nails – History
1. Table   11. Moss, Michael Stanley

ISBN 0-900673-16-8

Filmset in Monophoto Plantin
Printed and bound by Butler & Tanner Ltd, Frome and London
Published by Lang & Fulton, Greenock
Distributed by John Smith & Sons (Glasgow) Ltd,
57 St Vincent Street, Glasgow G2

Designed by Charles Carver

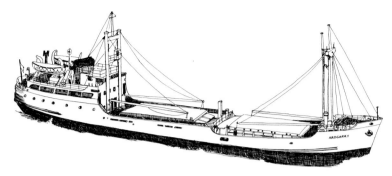

MV Ardgarry

Contents

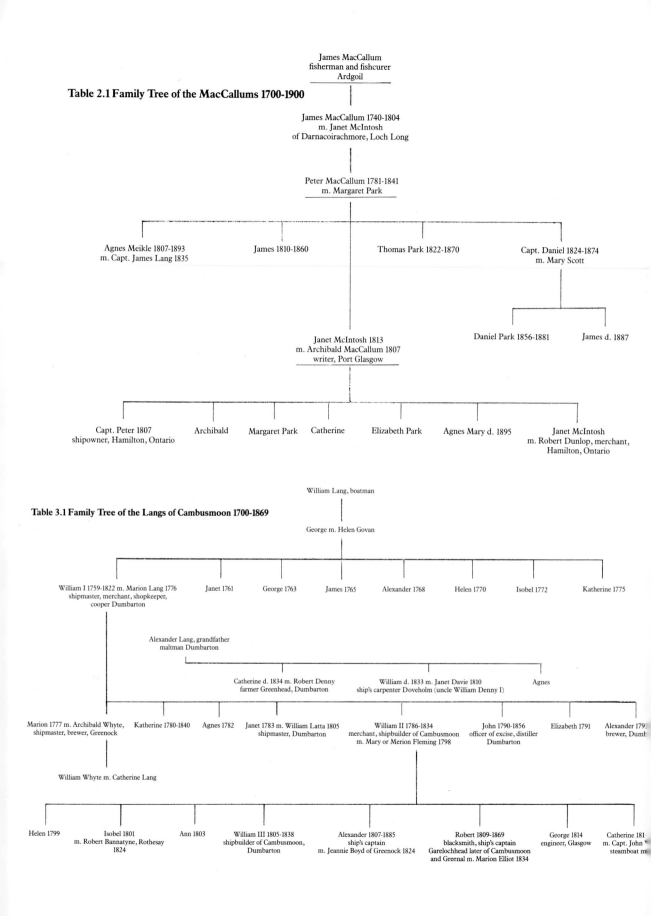

Table 2.1 Family Tree of the MacCallums 1700-1900

James MacCallum
fisherman and fishcurer
Ardgoil

James MacCallum 1740-1804
m. Janet McIntosh
of Darnacoirachmore, Loch Long

Peter MacCallum 1781-1841
m. Margaret Park

Agnes Meikle 1807-1893
m. Capt. James Lang 1835

James 1810-1860

Thomas Park 1822-1870

Capt. Daniel 1824-1874
m. Mary Scott

Daniel Park 1856-1881

James d. 1887

Janet McIntosh 1813
m. Archibald MacCallum 1807
writer, Port Glasgow

Capt. Peter 1807
shipowner, Hamilton, Ontario

Archibald

Margaret Park

Catherine

Elizabeth Park

Agnes Mary d. 1895

Janet McIntosh
m. Robert Dunlop, merchant,
Hamilton, Ontario

Table 3.1 Family Tree of the Langs of Cambusmoon 1700-1869

William Lang, boatman

George m. Helen Govan

William I 1759-1822 m. Marion Lang 1776
shipmaster, merchant, shopkeeper,
cooper Dumbarton

Janet 1761

George 1763

James 1765

Alexander 1768

Helen 1770

Isobel 1772

Katherine 1775

Alexander Lang, grandfather
maltman Dumbarton

Catherine d. 1834 m. Robert Denny
farmer Greenhead, Dumbarton

William d. 1833 m. Janet Davie 1810
ship's carpenter Doveholm (uncle William Denny I)

Agnes

Marion 1777 m. Archibald Whyte,
shipmaster, brewer, Greenock

Katherine 1780-1840

Agnes 1782

Janet 1783 m. William Latta 1805
shipmaster, Dumbarton

William II 1786-1834
merchant, shipbuilder of Cambusmoon
m. Mary or Merion Fleming 1798

John 1790-1856
officer of excise, distiller
Dumbarton

Elizabeth 1791

Alexander 179:
brewer, Dumb

William Whyte m. Catherine Lang

Helen 1799

Isobel 1801
m. Robert Bannatyne, Rothesay
1824

Ann 1803

William III 1805-1838
shipbuilder of Cambusmoon,
Dumbarton

Alexander 1807-1885
ship's captain
m. Jeannie Boyd of Greenock 1824

Robert 1809-1869
blacksmith, ship's captain
Garelochhead later of Cambusmoon
and Greenal m. Marion Elliot 1834

George 1814
engineer, Glasgow

Catherine 181
m. Capt. John
steamboat m

Foreword

by Dr Thomas R Craig, CBE, LLD, formerly chairman of Colvilles Ltd

I enjoy reading history and specially industrial history. I was pleased, therefore, that P MacCallum & Sons were producing a history of the first two hundred years of their existence. I knew this would cover a firm in the West of Scotland which had close links with my own career of steelmaking. I was sure such a history would provide the greatest interest and I have not been disappointed.

On reading, one general fact which has struck me is the tremendous amount of change which they have had to face. They started with wooden sailing ships, then wrought iron replaced the wood of the hulls and steam engines replaced the sails; iron gave place to steel and steam to diesel and there are many other changes.

Apart from those items which directly affected their business, they have lived through two centuries of invention and discovery. When they started there were no railways, no motors, no aeroplanes, no telegraph, no telephone, no wireless – even no penny post! To exist and develop during periods of such violent change was only made possible by the ability, foresight and courage of those in charge and here P MacCallum were fortunate in the representatives of the three families associated throughout its existence.

Naturally one of the parts of the history which gripped my attention was MacCallums involvement in the steel industry. Personally I had been in contact with them throughout my 50 years with the manufacturing side of the Scottish steel industry. MacCallums had four sides in their steel business: importing from abroad; supplying English and Welsh steel; buying and selling Scottish steel; and steel stockholding. In the first two of these they were fierce competitors. Figures quoted in this history show what a substantial tonnage they handled. Looking back it could be said that competition kept us on our toes and made us more efficient, but that was not how we felt then. I remember fighting them as hard as possible in an effort to reduce the extent of their market.

One pleasant feature of this period was that despite the obvious rivalry between the manufacturer and the trade the personal relationship between the principals was that of mutual respect. There never was the thought that either side would indulge in any shady dealing.

My personal contact was with Ian MacCallum Lang and this I am pleased to say went further than respect and was indeed friendly. I used to call on him personally in Greenock and although I did not always get the order for steel which I hoped for, I enjoyed the exchange of news and the discussion on industry in general. My memory of him is a very pleasant one.

This is the story of a unique family firm, which has already been in existence for over two hundred years, proving it has remarkable powers of adapting itself to constantly changing conditions. It has had its good times and its bad, but each generation has been determined to carry on. I am certain its present leaders have retained these powers so its continuation is assured.

List of Tables

Victorian Office

Preface and Acknowledgements

Our great industries have their historians; and the success stories of our country's largest companies are well documented. Yet the commercial skill which brought Great Britain prosperity at the height of the Empire, and continued well into the twentieth century, was founded not just on the giants that flourished (and sometimes failed) during that time, but far more on countless thousands of little businesses – industrious, adventurous, innovative and indispensable – which carved out their uncertain progress across a wide range of endeavour. This book is about one such business.

Too often the story of the myriad small firms that comprised the commercial backbone of Victorian Britain has gone untold. Few records survived: company and accounting law was less developed. Life for many enterprises was uncertain and often short. But P MacCallum & Sons Ltd have survived and we congratulate its directors on deciding to mark this, their bicentenary, with a history of their firm. We thank them for inviting us to write it.

It is a story of survival rather than growth, of hard work and modest living rather than driving ambition or flamboyance; a story of opportunities seized and setbacks overcome. It confirms that view now more widely accepted, that small can be beautiful and illustrates, from two centuries of experience, that the trade cycle of boom and recession is no new phenomenon. Rather, the unexpected blow is the norm and ought to be the expected.

Although in this book we tell the history of P MacCallum & Sons and the shipping firm Lang & Fulton that sprang from it and, after about fifty years, was re-absorbed into it, it could be the story of almost any small firm that traded during the period our story covers. MacCallums have the distinction of having endured now for over two hundred years, and for part of that time achieved prominence on the industrial scene, but the qualities that invested their survival are the same qualities that could have been seen in many another small company during the period. By laying out in some detail certain aspects of the iron and steel merchanting business, and the operation of a tramp shipping fleet, we have tried to place on record a commercial picture that must have been typical of many such companies since the industrial revolution and which might otherwise have been lost to history.

In writing this study we have received much kindness and assistance. We would like to thank Peter and Patricia Lang for their enthusiastic encouragement, their unearthing of yet more and more documents and photographs relating to the firm's past, and for their generous hospitality; Dr Tom Craig, for writing the foreword and giving of his extensive knowledge of the Scottish steel industry; Margaret Miller for listing the records of the firm and introducing us to Patricia Lang; John McLintock, whose skill in genealogical research made it possible to unravel the complexities of the Lang family tree and who unearthed much useful information about the early history of the business; Derek Mullins, who looked through the Greenock and Port Glasgow Registers of Shipping; Jim Emery, who helped search for references to the firm in records of the Scott-Lithgow group held in the Glasgow University Archives; Sir William Lithgow, who allowed us access to the Lithgow papers deposited at the University and held privately by himself, and made available the transcript of Joseph Russell's diary; Campbell McMurray, who explained the complexities of locating official crew lists and logs in the Board of Trades records; Trevor Neill of Harland & Wolff, who gave us access to the records of that firm and those of Workman Clark; to Graham E Langmuir for lending photographs from his unrivalled collection; to William Lind, who has given us much useful information about the Lang family drawn from his researches in the *Dumbarton Herald* and has made available photographs from his extensive collection; to William M Lang for providing information about his father, Archie Orr Lang; to Sir Percival Griffiths; to Donald Cameron for supplying information about his steel merchanting business; to Mr W Thomson of Wigham & Poland Ltd for giving information about Rose Murison & Thomson; to Mr T F Young for describing his early years in shipping insurance in Glasgow; to Rita Hemphill and Ruth Sirton for typing the manuscript; to Charles Carver for his excellent design, and to Lynne Bailie for sub-editing the text at breakneck speed.

All the illustrations have been provided by P MacCallum & Sons, with the exception of the drawings which are by John Hume and:

Title page	*G W Wilson collection, Aberdeen University Library*
2.4, 3.3, 4	*John R Hume*
3.1, 2, 5, 6, 4.2	*Graham E Langmuir collection*
4.1	*Scotts Shipbuilding and Engineering Co*
5.6, 7	*Sir William Lithgow, Bt.*

At the Tail of the Bank, 1981.

John R Hume

Michael S Moss

Table 3.2 Family Tree of the Langs of Chapeltown, Dumbarton 1750-1887

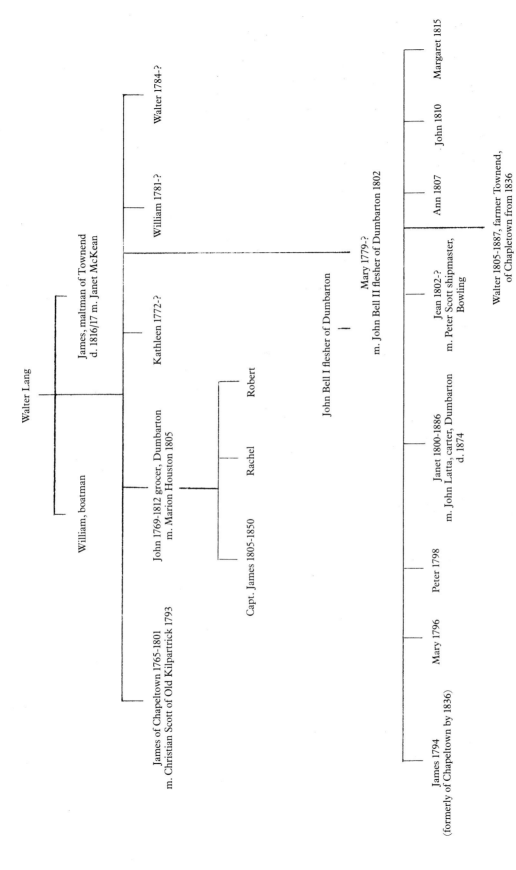

Table 4.1 Lang and Fulton Family Trees 1805-1981

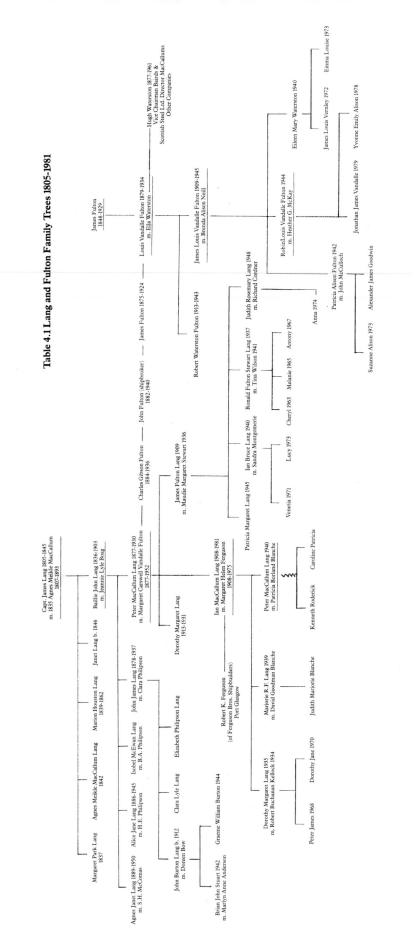

Custom House, Greenock

Chapter 1
Setting the Scene

The prosperity of Britain in the nineteenth century rested not only on its great commercial cities but on a large number of small towns in Northern England and Central Scotland. These towns had, and even in the late twentieth century still have, much in common. Their business communities were close knit and self-reliant. Their tradesmen and manufacturers shunned ostentation, only moving to larger villas in the final wash of fashion. This prudence was reflected in public building, whether by the local authority, the churches or other bodies. Public works essential for continued commercial success were undertaken only after lengthy debate and scrupulous consideration and often at the last moment, while public buildings were constructed usually out of necessity but with great reluctance. Consequently even in the 1980s these towns are often dominated by an ungainly late nineteenth century town hall and contain a number of nondescript churches of similar vintage and indistinguishable denomination. The humdrum provincial life of such towns has been brilliantly portrayed by Arnold Bennet in his novels about the five pottery towns of North Staffordshire. Yet despite or perhaps because of their outward tedium, these little towns produced in the nineteenth century more than their fair share of large businesses that became household names.

Their commercial success was a reflection of their smallness. Their businessmen, knowing each others strength and weaknesses, and the probity of their leading citizens operated their enterprises to mutual advantage, lending each other money to fund speculative ventures. During times of crisis they were prepared to help those who found themselves in difficulties through no fault of their own. However, those whose failure resulted from extravagance or inattention to their trade found no sympathy and their businesses were

1

allowed to pass into other hands. This cohesion and collusion in financial dealing required a backdrop of fiscal policy that encouraged the creation and transmission of capital from one generation to the other. After the introduction of death duties in 1894 and their dramatic rise in 1911 the fabric of these communities began to crumble as capital was dispersed and families drew money out of their businesses. Their death knell was sounded on the battlefields of Flanders. The holocaust, the great extension of war-related industry, large profits, inflation, and the good returns to be had from the war loan, formed an unlikely alliance to make many of the long-established commercial families in these towns finally lose their nerve and cash in their enterprises. The wisdom of their decision seemed to be confirmed in the long inter-war depression. The tale of decline and unfulfilled expectation thereafter is only too familiar.

Greenock on the lower reaches of the Clyde was and is just such a town, with its disproportionate half finished municipal building put up in the 1880s and its streets of workmanlike tenements and neat serviceable villas. From the late eighteenth century Greenock and adjacent Port Glasgow developed integrated commercial and manufacturing enterprises that quickly became self-supporting. During the course of the nineteenth century the two towns generated four powerful companies of international reputation; the Gourock Ropework Company and its sister concern, Birkmyre Brothers of Bombay; Scotts Shipbuilding and Engineering Co; Abram Lyle & Sons; and Russell & Co, later Lithgows Ltd. By the 1890s Russell & Co, established in 1874, had with little public acclaim or advertisement worked its way to the head of the list of Clyde shipbuilders when measured in terms of tonnage launched each year. Such unobtrusiveness was the hallmark of all four companies. Alongside and quite often under the shelter of those mighty concerns many little businesses flourished and grew, either supplying them with materials and services or in the same line of business. Many of these lesser concerns were established by men who had learnt their craft with the big four. Typically Russells helped these smaller firms with loans and orders and were themselves assisted by reciprocal investments in ships that they constructed.

Peter MacCallum & Sons, founded in the late eighteenth century, is characteristic of the smaller concerns that were essential to the great commercial wealth of Greenock and Port Glasgow between the mid-1880s and the outbreak of the First World War. It is unusual in that it is still based in Greenock and provides employment in the town. Lyles have long since moved to London, the Gourock ropeworks is closed and Scotts and Lithgows are nationalized with an uncertain future. Other Greenock firms that survive like Lyle Shipping Co and J & J Denholm, the ship owners, moved their offices to Glasgow many years ago and retain only tenuous links with their birthplace. What follows is the story of three families and their business in Greenock and how it has survived the vicissitudes of the trade cycle, war and government policy for two hundred years.

2

THE COMET, THE FIRST STEAM BOAT IN BRITAIN.
1811
Engraved by — — J. Swan Glas.

Henry Bell, Engineer,
Helensburgh.

Henry Bell's visiting card

Chapter 2

Peter MacCallum & Sons:
The First Hundred Years: to 1874

During the middle years of the eighteenth century, the Scottish economy began to expand rapidly. Glasgow and its ports of entry at the mouth of the Clyde – Greenock, Port Glasgow, and Dumbarton – flourished as its merchants came to dominate the tobacco trade with the American colonies. Until the Forth and Clyde Canal was opened in 1790, the tobacco was shipped to customers on the Continent or in Southern England coastwise: either north about Cape Wrath or south about Land's End. Trade with the Highlands also began to develop, as landowners there followed the fashion of estate improvement and the population increased. This was accompanied, particularly in Argyllshire and Ayrshire, by a dramatic rise in the smuggling of tobacco, tea, salt, continental wines and spirits and local whisky illicitly distilled. The expansion in coastal trade called into being in the lower Clyde ports of Greenock, Port Glasgow and Dumbarton a large boat-building industry with its attendant trades of timber merchanting, sawmilling, sail-making, brassfounding, block-making, rope-making and rigging. The boat builders gradually learned how to build and design technically advanced vessels. The smugglers, especially, needed very fast small boats, which could escape the revenue cutters and at the same time negotiate the small creeks and narrow channels of the west coast. Until the 1760s most of the ocean-going ships belonging to the Glasgow merchants had been built in America, but in 1764 Peter Love launched the first square rigged vessel to be constructed at Greenock, he was followed in 1765 by Walter McKirdy.[1]

The new-found wealth of Glasgow and its neighbouring towns attracted many people from the Highlands in search of work. Young men were apprenticed to craftsmen to learn such skills as handloom weaving, boat building, sugar making, and coopering. Young women came to work as servants in the homes of the prospering tradesmen and merchants. In 1740 James MacCallum was born at Ardgoil Farm near Ormidale in the parish of Kilfinnan on the Argyllshire shore of the Kyles of Bute. His father, also James, was a fisherman and fishcurer, catching the renowned Loch Fyne herring, either salting or kippering them, and sending them to the Glasgow market.[2] The young James MacCallum would have grown up amongst boats and boatmen, no doubt becoming only too familiar with the repair of small rowing and sailing boats used at 'the fishings' of the time. He would have seen the fishing industry in the Firth of Clyde grow quickly in the 1750s.

Like many of his contemporaries he went to Greenock to learn his trade, possibly boat building. Family tradition has it that some time in the mid-1760s he established a hardware business to supply copper and iron nails, ships furniture, mostly made from yellow metal, to the expanding boat and shipbuilding firms. The first record to survive of his business is a bill, apparently unpaid, dated 1782 – the year the British were forced to surrender to the American colonists at Yorktown. Sometime before this James Mac-Callum had married Janet McIntosh from Dornacoirachmore on Loch Long in Argyllshire, who had, perhaps, been in service in Greenock. It is not known how many children they had, but in 1781 their son Peter was born.

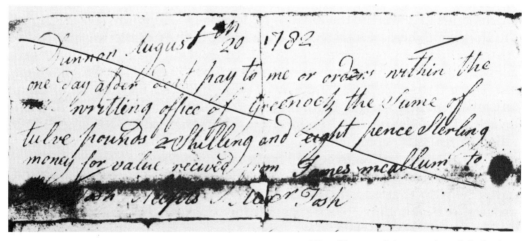

The oldest surviving mention of the business

By the turn of the century the Greenock shipbuilding industry was well established. The French revolutionary wars had brought fresh orders for large vessels, as West of Scotland merchants found it difficult to build their ocean-going ships in America. Nothing is known about the growth of James MacCallum's business between 1781 and his death in 1804. About 1800 his son, Peter, became a partner in the firm of Kennedy, Reid & MacCallum, iron merchants in Greenock. They were supplying the Greenock Foundry Co, a branch of the flourishing Scotts Shipbuilding Co, with bar iron in 1803 and 1804.[3] During 1803 Peter MacCallum went into partnership with John Graham to own and operate the 19-ton scow, *The Industry*, almost certainly for use in the rapidly developing herring fishing industry of the Firth of Clyde.[4] At his father's death, Peter MacCallum withdrew from the firm of Kennedy, Reid & MacCallum to take over the hardware business.

In the twenty years after 1805, Greenock's trade grew, despite the disruption caused by the Napoleonic wars. In 1805 – the year of Trafalgar – the new East India Harbour and its associated dry dock for ship repairing was opened.[5] By the mid-1820s Greenock had become the largest port in Scotland. In 1823 it had 249 registered vessels, compared with its nearest rival, Aberdeen, with 200 ships.[6] The pattern of its trade had changed, the West Coast traffic had declined and foreign shipments had risen.[7] The shipbuilding industry was well established, constructing ocean-going ships, hulls for the recently introduced steam vessels, and small coastal craft. Scotts was reputed to have the 'most complete' yard in Scotland and in 1826 Robert Steel & Co, launched the *United Kingdom*, then 'the largest and most splendid steam vessel built in this country.'[8] Following the widescale introduction of steam-boats from the late 1810s, a marine engineering industry also developed in the town led by Scotts and Caird & Co. At the same time Dumbarton shipbuilding experienced a similar rise in its fortunes. (See pages 13 to 16.)

Although little information survives about Peter MacCallum's conduct of the family firm during these years, he seems to have shared in the increased prosperity of the town. In 1806 he married Margaret Park, daughter of Thomas Park, a local timber merchant who had died the previous year. Borrowing £400 from his father-in-law's estate in 1812, Peter MacCallum bought a house and buildings in which he seems to have installed nail-making and spike-making equipment.[9] He purchased an adjacent garden in 1814 and large house and office in Deer Park Street in 1817, which he extended in 1824.[10] Bigger premises were, presumably, required to meet the needs of his expanding hardware and nail-making business, particularly the supply of iron nails and spikes. During these years Henry Bell, the owner of the *Comet* – the first commercially successful steam vessel – is reported to have been a regular visitor to the warehouse.[11]

No details survive of Peter MacCallum's range of stocks at this time. D McLellan, a hardwarer in Glasgow, held an astonishing variety of goods in 1830, including pocket knives, scissors, snuff-boxes, spectacles, inkstands, soap brushes, teapots, corkscrews, razors, toothbrushes, nutmeg graters, tweezers, chains, tableware, sandpaper, caddies, rings, needles and looking-glasses.[12] As MacCallum was supplying shipowners as well as shipbuilders, it is likely he held a similar range of wares. Wooden ships required constant attention. Routine maintenance of the hull, spars and rigging was carried out by the crews whenever vessels were in harbour, and on every voyage storms

Greenock from the east, in 1829

could be expected, which would open seams, and damage sails and rigging, requiring immediate repair. To remain serviceable, ships needed to carry good stocks of nails, iron straps, sailmakers' needles and spare parts as well as goods necessary for the daily life of the crew. When Ewing, Miller & Co and Miller, Fergus & Co, two ship-owning firms in Greenock, failed in 1820, they owed Peter MacCallum £240 for goods. Norman McLeod, a ship-owner in the town, was sequestrated in 1828 owing him £300.[12] Between 1807 and 1824 Peter and Margaret MacCallum had a large family – Agnes Meikle (1807), James (1810), Janet McIntosh (1813), Peter (1815, died in childhood), Thomas Park (1822), and Daniel (1824). (See Table 2.1 on page vi.)

Peter MacCallum resumed his ship-owning ventures in 1814 when he acquired a vessel of 25 tons in association with Peter McLean, a cooper in Greenock, and Alexander McLean, a mariner there. In 1818 with Daniel McLean and Alexander McVicar he purchased a much larger vessel, the *Anna*, of 112 tons, possibly for use in foreign trade. He seems to have given up his interests in these vessels in the 1820s to concentrate on his expanding hardware business.[13]

By the early 1830s Peter MacCallum would seem to have built up a sizeable business on the lower reaches of the Clyde, supplying not only Greenock, but also Dumbarton. The extent of his trade can be gauged from his sales to, the shipbuilder, William Denny, owner of the Woodyard in Dumbarton (see page 14). In October 1833 he wrote to Denny:

'I have sent you
5 baskets 6   inch spikes
5 baskets 7   inch spikes
3 baskets 5½ inch spikes
2 baskets 5   inch spikes
15 baskets to be returned: which makes:

15 baskets of spikes @ 16/- - £12: -: –
15 baskets of spikes @   1/- -: 15: –

> I will *with your permission* send next week 15 baskets more in having no 6 or 7 inch nails made for you as iron is advanced. Spikes and nails must also advance and I have charged you the same as formerly & will send you 3 tons of them at the same price for you will find the prices in England and in East of Scotland to meet the above price now. They get their nails much cheaper than we do here, by their workmen which operate against me. We think ours are better made and not so thick that you can have a *greater number* in *the same weight*. I can supply you with Bar and Bolt iron at £7-15 shillings per ton. Please to write me about the spikes and your orders also for iron. Will much oblige.'[14]

MacCallum's concern at English competition refers to the recent introduction of mechanized nail-making machinery (particularly by Birmingham manufacturers) which resulted in massive unemployment amongst hand-nailers.[15] MacCallum must have installed such equipment shortly after this so as to remain in business. During March 1834 Peter MacCallum sent Denny one hundredweight of deck nails, two hundredweights of 5½ inch spikes, seven hundredweights of 6 inch spikes, and two hundredweights of 7 inch spikes.[16]

In 1838 Peter MacCallum took his sons James and Thomas Park into partnership to form the firm of Peter MacCallum & Sons. He also conveyed all his property to his children to be held in trust for them.[17] His youngest son, Daniel, entered the shipping industry, becoming master of the steamship *Ethiopia*. His eldest daughter, Agnes Meikle MacCallum, married Captain James Lang of the Dumbarton Steamboat Company in 1835 (see page 20). At about the same time his other daughter, Janet McIntosh MacCallum, married Archibald MacCallum, a writer or lawyer in Greenock.

The hulls of early steam ships were made of wood. However, the movement which is always present in wooden vessels caused repeated damage to engines and their associated propelling machinery. From the late 1820s experiments were conducted in the use of iron hulls. The first shipyard to specialize in the construction of iron hulled ships was started in 1836 by Tod & MacGregor at Springfield, Stobcross, not far from the centre of Glasgow.[18] Iron hulls were quickly adopted for steamships as their greater rigidity was ideal for bearing engines, paddle wheels, and later shafts and propellers. However, they were too expensive for most forms of merchant sailing ships and unsuitable for ships trading in tropical waters until the development of effective anti-fouling paint in the late 1850s.[19] Although the engineer-shipbuilders in Greenock, like Caird & Co and Scotts Shipbuilding

& Engineering Co, began building iron steamships in the 1840s, most of the firms there continued to construct wooden ships of all types.[20]

It is not known when Peter MacCallum & Sons began supplying iron ship plates. The available evidence suggests that throughout the 1840s and into the 1850s the firm continued to deal principally in nails, spikes, bar and bolt iron and, copper and yellow metal fittings, for which there must have been considerable demand. Probably, for this reason, it did not win the custom of

William Denny II who began iron shipbuilding at Dumbarton in 1844.[21] As shipbuilding, particularly that of merchant ships, has always been an uncertain industry, bankruptcies were frequent during the whole of the nineteenth century. Peter MacCallum & Sons appear as creditors in nearly all the bankruptcy records of Greenock shipbuilders in the 1840s, showing that the firm was, perhaps, the chief supplier of shipbuilding nails in the town. For example, when James McMillan's yard failed in 1843 it owed Peter MacCallum & Sons £118.[22] As nearly all shipbuilding subcontractors were paid by means of bills of exchange drawn by the supplier on the customer and rarely discounted, Peter MacCallum stood to lose every time a shipyard closed. It is a tribute to his business acumen that his firm was not pulled down by one of these failures.

In 1854 – the year the Crimean War was declared – Peter MacCallum died at the age of seventy-three. He left, besides his property, the relatively large sum of £5,970, of which £2,000 was loaned to Greenock Corporation. The balance was made up of debts due from his customers, which included the Greenock Distillery Co, Denny & Rankin, shipbuilders in Dumbarton, William Fyfe & Co, ship chandlers in Greenock, Robert Steel & Co, shipbuilders in Greenock, William Denny & Brothers, shipbuilders in Dumbarton, John Scott & Sons of Greenock, John Donald, boatbuilder in Greenock, and John Buchanan Junior & Co, coopers in Greenock. His estate was divided equally between his children.[23] His eldest son, James MacCallum, became senior partner of Peter MacCallum & Sons, which he continued to manage with his brother, Thomas Park MacCallum. They were joined by their nephew, John Lang, who had come to live in Greenock along with his mother and sisters after the death of his father, Captain James Lang, in 1850 (see page 23).

Almost immediately the firm began to deal in iron plate, winning large contracts from Scotts Shipbuilding & Engineering Co, who, although they had begun building iron ships in the 1840s, only switched predominantly to iron in the mid-1850s. By 1858 MacCallums were supplying between £500 and £1,500 worth of iron to Scotts each month.[24] Because of the large

Thomas Park MacCallum in his middle years

numbers of iron works that had opened in the West of Scotland and the rest of Britain in the 1840s and 1850s for the manufacture of ship plates, firms like Scotts preferred to buy their plate through a merchant rather than deal with the producers direct. For the shipbuilder this ensured keen prices, relieved him of the difficult problem of transporting the plates, and allowed for long credit, since the merchant paid the producer by bill and was paid by bill by his customers. In entering the bulk iron trade, Peter MacCallum & Sons became more of a merchanting than a stockholding concern. Very little of the plate the firm dealt in would ever have actually passed through its stockyard. Other Greenock ship-builders began constructing iron ships in the mid-1850s and almost certainly drew some of their supplies from Mac-Callums. Nevertheless, wood still remained the most popular material for merchant ships and demand for nails, spikes and bar and bolt iron must have remained high.

The blacksmith's shop of George Currie & Sons, Sand-bank established in 1851, photographed in 1972. This firm has been a customer of MacCallums from the earliest years.

James MacCallum died in 1861, leaving £1,362. Of this, £840 represented his third share of the firm of Peter MacCallum & Sons, giving it a total value of about £2,500, roughly the same as the small shipyards on the Lower Clyde at the time.[25] As James MacCallum was a bachelor, his property passed to his brother, Thomas Park MacCallum, who became the senior partner of the business. During the 1860s the pattern of the firm's trade seems to have continued much as before, possibly with some increase in its iron plate business.

In 1867 Thomas Park MacCallum became involved in shipowning with his nephew, Peter MacCallum, son of his brother-in-law, Archibald MacCallum. The family had helped Archibald MacCallum set up a business as a writer in Greenock, advancing him money against his share in Peter MacCallum's estate. When his firm had got into difficulties in 1856, they agreed to compound their loan of £800 at the rate of sixpence in the £1.[26] They had assisted his eldest son Archibald, later Procurator Fiscal of Greenock, to join his father in a new legal firm. They also gave help to Archibald MacCallum's other children including Peter MacCallum who, like his uncle Daniel, was a ship's master. Captain Peter emigrated to Canada and, with the aid of a loan of nearly $6,400 from his uncle, Thomas Park MacCallum, he had built in 1867 a 196-ton schooner named *Persia* at Hamilton, Ontario. The business did not prosper and failed in 1869.[27]

Thomas Park was equally unlucky in another venture. In 1861 he loaned William Smith & Co, engineers and ironfounders in Greenock £1,500 presumably to help finance their business.[28] This was followed by a further loan of £700 in 1866.[29] In 1868 the business collapsed and was acquired for a nominal sum by Hastie, Kincaid & Donald, also engineers and founders in the town.[30] The late 1860s was a time of severe depression, intensified by the failure of Overend & Gurney, the London bankers, in 1867. Greenock was badly hit with Scotts Shipbuilding & Engineering Co suspending payment in 1868,[31] and other firms like William Smith & Co going out of business. Joseph Russell, manager of the Inchyard at Port Glasgow, noted in his diary for the year: 'nothing doing in yard and finances in a critical state ... No journeymen in yard except two joiners – no labourers'.

In 1869 Thomas Park MacCallum died suddenly, while travelling on a horse drawn omnibus in Greenock. He left £2,900 of which £2,611 represented his seven-tenths share in the firm of Peter MacCallum & Sons. His inventory showed that apart from venturing capital in risky loans, he had also invested in two shares in the Campbeltown Bread & Flour Co, four shares in the London, Chatham & Dover Railway, five shares in the Atlantic Telegraph Co, and five shares in the United Kingdom Telegraph Co.[32] Thomas Park, like his brother James, died a bachelor and his property passed to his brother, Captain Daniel MacCallum, who was content to remain a sleeping partner. With a loan of £600 from his uncle, Captain Daniel, John Lang became an equal partner in the firm,[33] which he managed with the help of the head clerk, James Fulton. At the same time Daniel Park MacCallum, Captain Daniels's eldest son, then aged fourteen, entered the business with a view to becoming a partner. Captain Daniel died at Bombay in 1874 leaving just over £1,000.[34] As Daniel Park was unwell he seems to have retired and sold his share in Peter MacCallum & Sons to James Fulton.[35]

The business was now nearly one hundred years old. Although it had not grown exceptionally fast since its foundation, it had survived, unlike many of its customers and competitors. Small firms like that of Peter MacCallum &

Sons have left few records of their first century in business, yet they contributed as much to the industrialization of Britain in this period as the well-known concerns such as Boulton & Watt or the New Lanark Cotton Mills.

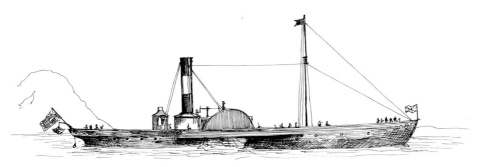

PS Dumbarton

Chapter 3

James Lang of Dumbarton: 1805–1850

On 18 January 1805 Marion Houston, an unmarried serving girl, was summoned before the Kirk Session of Dumbarton accused of being with child. She confessed that the father was her employer, John Lang, a grocer in the town.[1] She was rebuked. During April they were married in the neighbouring parish of Cardross.[2] Their child, James III, would seem to have been born shortly afterwards. It is not known how many children the couple had. There were certainly a second son, Robert, who died after choking on a piece of tripe, and two daughters, one of whom married Robert Hill of Greenock, owner of the River Line of ships.[3]

John Lang came from a family of maltsters at Townend of Dumbarton since the early eighteenth century. (See fig. 3.2 on page xi.) His father, James I, made sufficient capital in the malt trade to enable him to purchase the farm of Chapelton on the outskirts of Dumbarton in 1780 – the year of the Gordon riots.[4] John's eldest brother, James II, went into the family business taking over the maltings at Overbegs, Townend.[5] His sister, Mary, married John Bell, a flesher in the town, whose family came from Carlisle.[6] Nothing is known about his other brother and sisters. They possibly died in childhood.

The Langs of Chapelton were distantly related to the Langs of Cambusmoon whose members had become leading businessmen in Dumbarton by the early years of the nineteenth century. (See fig. 3.1 on page 16.) By 1800 William Lang I was an established shipowner, cooper and shopkeeper in the town with business interests in Port Glasgow.[7] His brother, George, was a grocer and his brother James, a merchant, who was known locally as James A'thing since he was prepared to tackle anything. In 1776 as the American colonies declared independence, William I had married Marion Lang, closely related to the Dennys who were laying the foundations of their shipbuilding and shipping enterprises.[8] Her brother, William Lang of Doveholm, had a size-able firm of ships' carpenters. He had learnt his trade in the Royal Navy.[9] His business almost certainly built small sailing boats for the West Coast trade. Between 1777 and 1793 William and Marion Lang had a large family.

In 1809 when James Lang III of the Chapelton family was four, his father John's grocery firm was sequestrated.[10] This was probably due to the very poor harvests in Scotland in the preceding two years, which had resulted in a ban during 1809 on the distillation of whisky, probably one of John Lang's main sales lines. Although his father stood cautioner for his debts, John Lang does not seem to have remained in business.[11] No record survives of his subsequent career or the date of his death. It is not possible to find out where James Lang III was educated. After he left school he became an apprentice law clerk in the office of the town clerk of Dumbarton.[12] At this time town clerks combined these positions with that of a legal practice. While serving his time James Lang would have learnt a good deal about book-keeping, office management and, not least, the law. He would have had regular contact with the leaders of the business community in Dumbarton and would have seen its industries, particularly shipbuilding, prosper in the early 1820s. Most strikingly he would have watched the rapid introduction of the paddle steam ship.

The first commercially viable steamboat, the *Comet*, had been built for Henry Bell in 1812. With its hull built on the Lower Clyde and its engines and boilers in Glasgow, it set a pattern in steamboat construction which persisted for nearly thirty years.[13] Shipbuilders in Dumbarton quickly copied Bell's example. In 1814 Archibald McLachlan, an established shipbuilder at Woodyard in the town, started constructing hulls for steamboats.[14] When McLachlan died in 1818, his business was taken over by his manager, William Denny I, who continued building steamships with considerable success. [15] He was joined in 1821 by James 'A'thing' Lang, who in 1811 had built at Dumbarton, one of the first privately owned drydocks 'for graving and repairing large vessels' and laid out an adjacent shipyard known as the Church Yard.[16] This was a propitious time to begin building big ocean-going vessels as the war with the United States, which broke out the following year, closed to British owners the American yards which had been their main source of new heavy tonnage. Lang probably drew on the shipbuilding experience of his relations to help him start his business. He began to con-struct very sizeable vessels. For example, the East Indian *Pestongee Bomagee* of 560 gross tons was delivered in about 1816.[17] Lang's first steamship was the *Comet II*, built in 1821 for Henry Bell as a replacement for the first *Comet* which had foundered.[18] Lang began by using engines supplied by Duncan McArthur who owned an engineering works at Camlachie in Glasgow. McArthur withdrew from business in 1822 and Lang switched for the supply of his engines to the celebrated cousins David and Robert Napier. David

14

Napier made his reputation when he designed the *Rob Roy*, which inaugurated the steamship service between Greenock and Belfast. This vessel was constructed in 1818 by William Denny and engined by Napier. Robert Napier started his own marine engineering business in 1821, when his cousin opened a large works at Lancefield on the Clyde in the middle of Glasgow. David and Robert Napier soon came to dominate the marine engineering industry of the West of Scotland. They must have been well known to James Lang as the family came originally from Dumbarton. David's father, John, had been an ironfounder and engineer in the town until he moved to Glasgow in 1802 and Robert's father had been a blacksmith. By 1832 Lang had become one of the most important builders of paddle steamers on the Clyde, having constructed fifteen of the fifty-nine vessels in service on the river – more than any other builder.[19]

Dumbarton Castle and town from Langbank in the 1820s

While James Lang was expanding his business, his brother, William II, the shipmaster, died in 1822. The following year his eldest son William III followed his uncle's lead when he took over the Cambusmoon shipyard from William Govan.[20] No records survive of the types of vessels built at Cambusmoon, but it is likely that they were coasting vessels of relatively small tonnage. The coastal trade grew rapidly in the late 1810s and early 1820s as industry expanded. In 1827 William's younger brother, John, who had become an excise officer, opened a new distillery at Bridgend of Dumbarton.[21]

Whisky making was flourishing following the introduction of stiff penalties against illicit distillers in 1822 and measures to encourage licensed operators in 1823. Although a great number of those who entered the industry in the 1820s subsequently withdrew, John Lang's business prospered until his retirement in 1857.[22] In the mid-1820s William's next brother, Alexander, opened a brewery in the town.[23]

James Lang III's apprenticeship as a clerk did not last long. On 15 May 1823 he was appointed steward on board the *Dumbarton*[24] which was owned by the Dumbarton Steamboat Company, whose partners included James A'thing Lang, his brother Alexander, a grocer, and his niece's husband, William Latta, a ship's carpenter.[25] These three men had established the company in 1815, immediately after the defeat of Napoleon at Waterloo, to operate the appropriately named *Duke of Wellington* to carry passengers and parcels up and down the Clyde from Dumbarton to Glasgow.[26] Investment in a steamship linking the town with its large up-river neighbour was an important adjunct to their other business interests. All of them were also ship-owners and involved in trading ventures. At the time Greenock, Port Glasgow and Dumbarton were the principal ports of entry for Glasgow, as the Clyde was not navigable for large vessels above Dumbarton. The Glasgow shipowners and shipbuilders who controlled the River Improvement Trust,

PS Duke of Wellington *the first steamboat of the Dumbarton Steamboat Company, off Dumbarton Castle*

resented the competition from Dumbarton and did their best to frustrate it by persuading the Trust to refuse the use of its piers and other facilities.[27]

James Lang III's duties as steward involved assisting the captain to collect the fares, instructing the passengers when to board and disembark, looking after the tableware and serving drink and food in the gentlemen's dining cabin. He was forbidden to take 'smuggled or illicit spirits on board the boat thereby the proprietors of the boat may be attached or brought to trouble.'[28] Under legislation passed in 1822, if illicit spirit was discovered on a vessel, the vessel could be seized by the Revenue. In 1826, at the age of twenty-one, James Lang III became master of the *Dumbarton*, now owned by the newly formed New Dumbarton Steamboat Company.[29] This concern was simply a reconstruction of the old company with a wider partnership and shortly adopted its name. Although no records survive of James Lang III's career between 1823 and 1826, it is likely that he was promoted from steward to pilot, probably in 1824. In this position he would have learned the art of navigating a steam boat in the shallow waters of the Clyde, which would have been essential for his appointment as Captain.

The position of master of a steamboat at the time involved not only the navigation of the vessel and disciplining of the crew, but also the maintenance of the hull and engines in good working order and the keeping of voyage accounts. The crew would have comprised a pilot, two or three seamen, an engineer, a fireman, a steward, a cook, and a boy.[30] During 1826 the Dumbarton Steamboat Company purchased the *Leven*, built by James Lang in

1821 and the first vessel ever to be engined by Robert Napier.[31] In 1828 after two years as master of the *Dumbarton*, Captain James Lang transferred to the *Leven*. Despite his short service with the company, the management committee were so impressed with 'his good conduct and attention' that it was agreed 'he should be allowed to share in the new steamboat or in the old concern'. He was allotted $\frac{1}{21}$ share in the *Leven, Dumbarton*, and in the *New Dumbarton*, under construction by James A'thing Lang at the Dockyard.[32]

The engine of the PS Leven, *preserved in the town centre, Dumbarton*

In 1827 Captain James Lang took on the additional job of ship's husband to *The Lady of the Lake* owned by the Loch Lomond Steamboat Company.[33] This enterprise had been established in 1825 by a group of Dumbarton businessmen, including Lang's uncle, John Bell I, and his son, John Bell II, to operate *The Lady of the Lake* in competition with David Napier's *Marion*, which had inaugurated steamer services on the loch in 1818. There followed a period of intense competition, with passengers being offered all sorts of inducements, such as free meals.[34] John Bell I did not live to see the result of his investments as he was killed on 21 October 1825 when the *Comet II* was sunk in collision with the *Ayr* with the loss of seventy lives.[35] In April 1826 the *Marion* hit *The Lady of the Lake* causing considerable damage. By 1827 the Loch Lomond Steamboat Company was in difficulties, with large debts.[36] Captain James Lang, it would seem, was offered the post of ship's husband in an effort to stem the losses. The 1827 season was disastrous and the company was forced into liquidation. A new company was formed – which only survived for a year. In 1828 the Dumbarton Steamboat Company came to an agreement with David Napier to carry passengers from Glasgow to Loch Lomond for excursions on his boats.[37]

Captain Lang remained in command of the *Leven* until 1836. During these years the *Leven* was engaged primarily in providing a regular service between Dumbarton and Glasgow, occasionally working on the link route from Helensburgh across to Greenock and thence to Dumbarton.[38] In the early 1830s competition was fierce. The *Dumbarton* made large losses between 1829 and 1830, while even the *New Dumbarton*, despite good returns, recorded losses in 1832 and 1833. The only boat that made consistent profits was the *Leven*.[39] In April 1830 it was decided to lay up the *Old Dumbarton* 'due to the competition among proprietors of different steamboat companies plying the Clyde reducing freights to below when adequate return is achieved.'[40] During June the company tried to enter the rapidly expanding holiday trade by opening a service to Arrochar using the *Old Dumbarton*. This was closed early in July as Captain Lang, as a shareholder, objected to the large losses that were being incurred.[41] The boat was sold. So as to remain in business the company reduced wages to five shillings a week for masters and engineers and two shillings for pilots, firemen and deckhands.[42] By 1834 the competition had waned and the company began to extend its service, re-opening the Arrochar route with the *Leven*.[43]

William Lang II of Cambusmoon died during 1834. His eldest son, William Lang III, took over his father's shipyard. His second son, Alexander, who had trained at the Dockyard with his great-uncle, James A'thing Lang, had been master of the paddle steamer *Dumbuck* since 1832, which was owned by the Dumbarton and Glasgow Steamboat Company in direct opposition to the Dumbarton Steamboat Company. His third son, Robert, was a smith in Dumbarton and his fourth son, an engineer in Glasgow. At his father's death Robert gave up his job as a smith and signed on with the Dumbarton Steamboat Company as steward on the *Leven*.[44]

The late 1830s were difficult times for industry in Dumbarton, as competition from Glasgow and Paisley, its up-river neighbours, intensified following the widening and deepening of the river. Since, at the time, it was common for steamship owners to order new vessels from the engineer rather than the shipbuilder, the opening of the shipyards on the upper river, near the major engineering works, was of particular concern to Dumbarton merchants. In 1835 their worst fears must have been confirmed when Tod & MacGregor, two of Robert Napier's foremen, opened their iron shipyard at

Stobcross, just downstream from Napier's engineering works.[45] This must have been a serious blow for James A'thing Lang who had established a strong connection with Robert Napier. The competition proved too great for him and during 1835 his business collapsed with debts of over £12,000. His creditors, chiefly suppliers of materials, included Pollock, Gilmour & Co, one of the largest Glasgow timber merchants, the Clyde Iron Works, Caird & Co of Greenock, the Crown Foundry, Port Glasgow; and Grainger & Evans, iron merchants of Neath, but not Peter MacCallum & Sons. The list of his debtors showed that he had been giving credit widely to his customers. He was owed money for at least twenty vessels, ranging from paddle steamers, through lighters and sloops, to scows.[46]

In 1835 Captain James Lang married Agnes, Peter MacCallum's daughter. He probably met her as a result of her father's business contacts with the Dumbarton shipbuilders. Their only son, John, was born the following year. There were also four daughters of the marriage, Margaret Park born 1837, Marion Houston, 1839 (died 1842), Agnes Meikle 1842 and Janet 1843.

Captain James Lang was appointed master of the new 112-ton *Vale of Leven* in 1835.[47] This vessel had been built of iron by Tod & MacGregor with engines by Robert Napier. It was a challenging post, as the *Vale of Leven* was only the second iron steamer to trade on the river. He was succeeded as skipper of the *Leven* by Robert Lang, who had joined as steward two years before. Such rapid promotion was common at the time, as there was a shortage of seamen with sufficient engineering knowledge to take command of steamboats. As master of the *Leven* he competed directly with his brother on the *Dumbuck*. A fierce rivalry developed. It is recounted that:

> 'Captain Robert Lang carried a piper on board his craft. One day when the rival steamers were racing quite close to each other Captain Robert's piper stepped out on to the paddle box of Captain Alexander's steamer and skirled on his pipes in ear-splitting, derisive style. Captain Alexander, who was a great wag, gave a quiet hint to his pilot to steer off from the other vessel, and so he captured his brother's piper, at which he laughed consumedly.'[48]

The year 1837, when Queen Victoria ascended the throne, was momentous too for Captain Lang. The failure of James A'thing Lang had left a gap not only in the capital, but also in the management of the Dumbarton Steamboat Company. Owing to protracted legal proceedings, his affairs did not begin to be settled until 1837. In May of that year his nephew Alexander, the brewer, and Captain Robert Lang, his great nephew, together with Captain James Lang, took over the direction of the firm.[49] In earnest of his new responsibilities and recent marriage, Captain James Lang purchased for £450 Horsewood House, Kilbarchan to the south of the Clyde.[50] He probably made his way to Dumbarton by going over the hills to Port Glasgow and taking a boat across the river.

Captain James Lang did not remain master of the *Vale of Leven* for long. In 1838 he took command of the new iron steamer *Loch Lomond*,[51] which seems also to have been built for the company by Tod & McGregor. While master of the vessel Captain James Lang was challenged by Captain James McLintock of the *Maid of Leven*, owned by the Dumbarton and Glasgow Steamboat Company, to a race between Greenock and Rothesay for a bet of £50.[52] Such competitions were popular at the time and the directors willingly allowed Captain Lang to take part. The outcome is not known.

During 1840 the company took delivery of a new steamer named *Prince Albert* in honour of the Queen's marriage that year. This was again built by Tod & McGregor, but with engines supplied by Thomas Wingate & Co of Glasgow.[53] Captain James Lang took command, serving as master for five years. In association with a sister ship, *Dumbarton Castle*, the *Prince Albert*

Silver salver presented to Captain James Lang in 1848,
when he ceased to command the Prince Albert.

provided a service three times a day from Glasgow to Dumbarton and back. The fare was sixpence cabin and twopence steerage.[54] During this time the company extended its excursion business. Captain James Lang came to be 'beloved by the school children of the town for he used to give them every now and again free trips "doon the watter" '.[55] On leaving the vessel in 1848 the townspeople of Dumbarton showed their appreciation by presenting him with 'a fine gold watch and appendages, also a silver kettle and various other pieces of plate, "in token of their estimate of his abilities and his uniform kind and gentlemanly conduct to passengers" '.[56]

During 1844 the Dumbarton Steamboat Company contracted with William Denny II to build his first steamer, the *Loch Lomond*. Constructed at Denny's new Kirkyard, the *Loch Lomond* was clinker built of iron, with flush rivets. The engines were supplied by Smith & Roger of Glasgow and her fittings incorporated some machinery and the anchor from the *Vale of Leven*.[57] At the suggestion of Captain James Lang, an iron engine room indicator was installed to allow the master or the pilot to communicate with the engineer. Formerly instructions had been passed to the engine room by kicking the engine room casing. Alexander Livingston, the pilot on the *Prince Albert*, had improved on this method by using a wooden baton. The new indicator 'was considered a great advance upon former methods and it was speedily adopted by owners of steamboats at home and abroad'.[58]

In the mid-1840s the three companies competing for the Glasgow and Dumbarton trade, the Dumbarton Steamboat Company, the Dumbarton and Glasgow Steamboat Company and the Clyde and Leven Steamboat Company, were threatened by proposals to open a railway between the two towns. The Greenock trade had been badly damaged since 1841 when the Glasgow, Paisley and Greenock railway opened. In 1846, to meet the challenge and to halt wasteful competition, the three companies amalgamated to

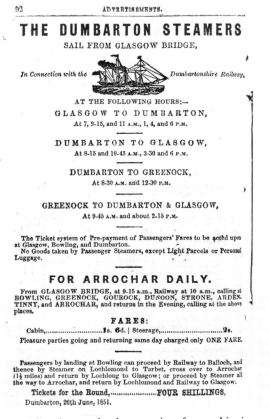

Advertisement for the operation of steamships in connection with the Dumbartonshire Railway in 1851

form the Dumbarton United Steamboat Company, later changed to the Dumbarton Steam Navigation Company.[59] As part of this plan the New Loch Lomond Steamboat Company was formed at the same time to take over the *Waterwitch* from the bankrupt business of McBrayne & M'Indoe, which had operated services on Loch Lomond for about ten years. This initiative was inspired by a shareholder, John Bell II, in the defunct firm. Bell was Captain Lang's cousin and a shareholder in the original concern. Lang took shares in the company and was appointed a director in 1848.[60] The new company's services were operated in close association with those of the Dumbarton United Steamboat Company.

In the event the railway between Glasgow and Dumbarton was not finished until the mid-1850s. However, the Dumbarton United Steamboat Company remained alive to the threat, coming to an arrangement with the railway to provide linking services with the half completed line from Dumbarton to Bowling in 1849,[61] and ordering two new steamers from William Denny, the *Queen* and the *Prince Albert*. The *Queen* was delivered early in 1850 and Captain James Lang appointed master.[62] However, he did not enjoy his new command for long. He died of cancer of the stomach at Castleroad House, Dumbarton, on 15 June at the age of forty-five.

He left his wife a modest fortune of about £3,000 along with his house at Kilbarchan. This included thirty shares in the Clydesdale Bank, forty shares in the City of Glasgow Bank, five shares in the Loch Lomond Steamboat Company, one share of the Dumbarton Steamboat Company, ten shares in the Clyde and Leven Steamboat Company, one hundred shares in the Glasgow Equitable Life Company and twenty shares in the North of Scotland

A group of old Dumbartonians at Dumbarton Quay in 1851, with many of John Lang's friends in front of his last steamer, the Queen

Life Insurance Company. He held £1,000 on short-term deposit with the Glasgow Current Exchange Company. He stipulated that his interest in the Dumbarton Steamers should be transferred to his son on his majority. He appointed as his trustees, Peter MacCallum, iron merchant in Greenock; John Bell, flesher in Dumbarton; Archibald MacCallum, writer in Port Glasgow; and James MacCallum.[63]

This tale of Captain James's career, like that of Peter MacCallum, is representative of those of others who lived in the West of Scotland during the second phase of the industrial revolution. Men like them played as important a role in laying the foundations for the commercial and industrial success of the West of Scotland in the late nineteenth century as heroes like Robert and David Napier. They are, though, largely forgotten. Yet it was probably their example and success that eventually made the West of Scotland the Workshop of the British Empire.

Loch Lomand PS *with Captain James Lang on the bridge.*

24

Melting shop at Colvilles

Chapter 4

**Through Iron to Steel –
Peter MacCallum & Sons: 1874 to 1919**

The year 1874 was not a good time for John Lang to take over as senior partner of Peter MacCallum & Sons. There was a serious depression in the shipping and shipbuilding industries which drove several Lower Clyde yards out of business, sometimes with consequential losses to the firm. For example, in 1874 Macfadyen & Co of the Bay Yard, Port Glasgow, collapsed with debts of over £18,000.[1] MacCallums were fortunate only to be owed £57. However, there were reassuring auguries for metal merchants. The price of iron plates had fallen and their quality was improving as newer and larger mills came into production. This, coupled with the termination of the patent held by John Elder & Co of Glasgow over the compound engine, made steam vessels viable for use in the premier cargo trades. Tramp ship owners were also attracted by the cheapness of iron into ordering big sailing vessels with iron hulls, masts and spars, which they hoped would be less expensive to operate than their wooden counterparts. In 1874 a new partnership of James Russell, Anderson Rodger and William Todd Lithgow took over the Bay Yard in Port Glasgow with a view to constructing such ships. From the outset they placed some of their orders for iron plate with Peter MacCallum & Sons.[2]

During the 1870s iron replaced wood as the chief shipbuilding material for all but the smallest craft. As a result MacCallums began to deal in quantity in iron plates, angles and stanchions, winning custom from all the Greenock and Port Glasgow shipyards and engineering works.[3] The supply of iron on a big scale transformed the business, enlarging its capital requirements to finance the large bills that had now to be drawn on individual customers. The premises in Deer Park Street, which had met the firm's needs since the 1820s, had to be extended by the purchase of several adjoining pieces of ground between 1876 and 1878.[4] In addition to iron, the firm continued to supply copper and yellow metal fittings (presumably used mostly for repairing wooden ships), copper tubing and yellow metal ingots. Since the local market for these materials was contracting, MacCallums came to an arrangement with Pascoe Grenfell & Sons, metal merchants of London to meet their requirements for copper and yellow metal items.[5]

John Lang senior partner of Peter MacCullam & Sons
from 1874 to 1903

In 1876 John Lang married Jeannie Lyle Boag, the daughter of a local businessman. Their first son, Peter MacCallum, was born in 1877, followed by a second, John James, the next year. There were also three daughters – Isobel McEwan, Alice Jane, and Agnes Janet. John Lang's partner, James Fulton, had married some time before. His first child, James Fulton, was born in 1875, followed by Margaret Carsewell Vandalle in 1877, Louis Vandalle in 1879, John Fulton, 1882, and Charles Gibson, 1884. (See fig. 4.1 above.)

In 1878 the risks attendant in supplying iron in quantity were only too forcibly impressed upon John Lang when the Cartsdyke yard of John Scott & Sons collapsed with debts of nearly £30,000 and assets of only £13,500. Scott owed MacCallum nearly £4,000 on four bills. He had started the business in 1873 and although he had secured a number of contracts, he had never given much attention to his company's financial affairs. The failure of the firm had been precipitated by the construction, for Lewis Potter & Co, of

26

Ocean King which had been completed in 1878, but remained unpaid for. This was because the principal of the firm, Lewis Potter had been arrested on charges of fraud in connection with the bankruptcy in 1878 of the City of Glasgow Bank of which he was a director. This bank was an unlimited joint stock bank, whose shareholders were required to meet the liabilities in full even though its directors had deliberately defrauded them.

There were 1,249 shareholders in the bank, most of whom owned relatively small parcels of stock. Shortly after the bank's liquidation, a fund was established to help shareholders, who faced personal bankruptcy as a result of the calls. John Lang's father, James, had left £855 worth of stock in the bank in the hands of his trustees who became liable for any calls on the stock. When the liquidation proceedings were completed in the early 1880s, each shareholder had paid some £2,750 on every £100 share.[7] Trustees could only meet these demands as far as their funds would allow. James Lang's trustees had only £2,300, which included £600 loaned to John Lang against the security of the shares in the Dumbarton Steamboat Company transferred to him on his majority in 1857. The funds were forfeited and the trust disbanded.[8] These were heavy blows for John Lang to receive so soon after

The iron stockyard at Scott's Cartsburn shipbuilding yard, Greenock, c. 1880, with the ornamental chimney of the Garvel graving dock in the background

taking charge of Peter MacCallum & Sons. In order to repay the loan to the trustees and provide the firm with working capital, he raised £1,800 in mortgages.[9] However, he was fortunate when compared with others. If he had owned the stock himself, he would have had to pay nearly £20,000, which would have ruined him. For example Joseph Russell, senior partner in the newly formed Russell & Company, had to find about £10,000 to cover his investment.[10]

As the economy recovered in the early 1880s, the market for iron increased rapidly, so enabling Peter MacCallum & Sons to overcome its problems. At

Russell & Company's Bay Yard, Port Glasgow, in the 1870s

Greenock and Port Glasgow the shipbuilding and marine engineering industries prospered. Scotts Shipbuilding & Engineering Co and Robert Duncan & Co (founded in 1863) expanded. Russell & Co took over the defunct Cartsdyke yard in 1879 and opened the new Kingston yard in 1883. It soon turned out a greater tonnage of ships each year than any other business on the river. These three concerns shortly became MacCallums' largest customers.

During the 1880s shipbuilders throughout the world began to switch from iron to open hearth steel. The open hearth process had been introduced to Scotland by the Steel Company of Scotland, founded in 1872. In 1877 Lloyd's published rules for building in steel, and after a few small craft had demonstrated the virtues of the new material, William Denny & Brothers

28

completed in 1879 the ocean-going *Rotomahana*. In 1879 and 1880 the well established West of Scotland iron-making firms of William Beardmore & Co, the Mossend Iron Company, David Colville & Sons and John Williams & Co, all installed open hearth furnaces.[12] Equivalent investments were made at the same time by iron firms in England and Wales and, more significantly, on the continent and in America. The iron industry in Germany and Belgium, which both had large reserves of minette ores that made a high phosphorus pig, quickly took advantage of the basic technique. German producers, defended by a tariff barrier that allowed them to sell cheaply into foreign markets, were soon acknowledged as world leaders in the manufacture and marketing of basic steel.[13]

Between 1879 and 1882 many Clyde shipyards experimented in constructing steel ships, but were deterred from further investigation by the depression in the industry which lasted from 1884 to 1887. It was not until the market improved in late 1887 that steel was adopted on a wide scale. By this time the price of steel had fallen below that of iron.[14] Russell & Co, for example, built their first steel ship in 1880 and invested in equipment to handle the larger steel plates, but did not build another steel ship until 1888, when they abandoned iron completely.[15]

At first the steel makers sold their steel direct to the shipyards. As demand rose and the number of producers grew, the shipbuilders began to buy at least some of their steel from metal merchants. In the mid-1890s, for example,

The melting shop of David Colville & Sons' Dalzell Steel-
works, Motherwell, in about 1890, with hand-charged open
hearth furnaces

Russell & Co had an account with the Lanarkshire Steel Co as well as with Peter MacCallum & Sons.[16] It was not known when Peter MacCallum & Sons first began dealing in steel, but by 1890 they were supplying Scotts Shipbuilding & Engineering Co.[17] The firm quickly established strong links with the major Scottish steel making concerns, Mossend Iron & Steel Co, Clydesdale Iron & Steel Co, David Colville & Sons, Clydebridge Steel Co, the Steel Company of Scotland, and Lanarkshire Steel Co. Some of these suppliers would have been well known to John Lang and James Fulton as manufacturers of iron plates and angles. In 1897, the first full year for which complete records of purchase and sales survive, MacCallums bought 10,830 tons of steel, equivalent to just under 2 per cent of the total make of steel ingots in Scotland. (See Table 4.3 on page 31.) Apart from buying steel from local producers, they were also drawing supplies from Consett Iron Co of Northumberland which was quoting equivalent prices. Their major customers were Robert Duncan & Co, Scotts Shipbuilding & Engineering Co, and Russell & Co.[18] (See Table 4.4 on page 32.)

Between 1898 and 1900 Clyde shipbuilding experienced its greatest boom of the century fuelled by Government expenditure on the South African war. MacCallum's purchases trebled in 1898 to just over 30,000 tons, retreated in 1899, and collapsed in 1900. Sales followed a similar trend. This reflected the rapid advance in the price of steel from about £5.50 a ton in 1898 to over £8 a ton by 1900 caused by increased demand and a consequent shortness in

A folding stock list of MacCallums, probably dating from the 1890s, but overstamped Limited in 1907, suggesting that the importance of this side of the business was receding

Table 4.2 Gross tangible assets and profits of Peter MacCallum & Sons, 1900–7

Date	Profit	Gross Tangible Assets	1 as a % of 2
1901	7,481	51,202	14.6
1902	3,247	54,309	5.98
1903	1,913	28,801	6.64
1903[1]	1,037	31,741	3.27
1904[1]	1,611	20,491	7.86
1905	3,526	29,916	11.79
1906	5,801	34,916	16.61
1907	7,673	84,886	11.83
1908	3,960	52,307	7.57

[1] *Half year.*
Abstracted from private ledger No. 6.

supply.[19] Clearly John Lang and James Fulton were not keen to buy at inflated prices and run the risk of a large loss. Moreover they were busy expanding their burgeoning shipowning business to take advantage of the high freight rates (see page 00). During 1899 as an experiment they purchased 21 tons of steel from the Carnegie Steel Co of America for £6.05 a ton. This was followed in 1900 by an order for 2,000 tons of ship plates at £7 a ton, well below the price quoted by Scottish manufacturers.[20] As the partners had probably guessed, the price of steel began to slide early in 1901 as new steel plants came into commission. Between 1898 and 1900 David Colville & Sons installed five new 50-ton furnaces (they had only 40-ton furnaces before) and a new plate rolling mill, and the Lanarkshire Steel Co spent nearly £250,000 on new plant.[21] During 1901 MacCallums' purchases advanced to 32,022 tons, all but 210 tons being ordered from Scottish manufacturers. This represented nearly $3\frac{1}{2}$ per cent of the total Scottish ingot make. Sales increased with Scotts taking 12,100 tons and Duncans 5,300 tons.[22] The profits for the year were £7,481, a yield of 14.6 per cent on the gross tangible assets of £51,000 (see Table 4.4 above).[23]

In 1899 Peter MacCallum Lang had become a partner in the firm at the age of twenty-three. The capital of the firm which then stood at £8,500 was reconstructed, John Lang holding 36/85ths, James Fulton 34/85ths and Peter MacCallum Lang 15/85ths.[24] Following the end of the Boer War, shipping freights fell swiftly and demand for new tonnage dwindled. MacCallums were badly hit with steel purchases dropping to 4,150 tons and profits being cut by a half.[25] The position would have been more serious had not the ship owning side of the business placed a contract with Russell & Co for the construction of a ship for which MacCallums were to supply the steel. (See page 52.) Sales improved slightly in 1903, but only at the expense of profits which retreated to under £2,000. (See Table 4.2 above.) In the midst of these difficulties, John Lang died at the age of sixty-seven. Shortly before, his partnership with James Fulton had been cemented by the marriage of his son Peter MacCallum, to Margaret Carswell Vandalle Fulton. By the time of his

Table 4.3 P MacCallum & Sons – Steel purchases in tons: 1896–1919

Date	From Scotland	From England and Wales (with Port Talbot purchases in ())		From Belgium	From Germany	From USA	Total	Total as % of total Scotland Ingot make
1896[1]	9,203	1,600					10,803	1.85
1897	9,530	1,300					10,830	1.35
1898	31,226						31,226	3.3
1899	18,051	50			20	21	18,121	1.9
1900	2,293					2,000	4,293	0.45
1901	31,812				210		32,022	3.4
1902	4,130	20					4,150	0.41
1903	14,229						14,229	1.57
1904	18,075	500		700			19,275	1.76
1905	56,787	160		500			57,447	4.53
1906	25,836	2,000[2]					27,836	2.13
1907	29,435	750[2]					30,185	2.35
1908	6,141	32,964	(10,000)	850	3,000[2]		69,325	6.74
1909	64,220	22,865	(11,000)	600	3,250[2]		90,935	8.81
1910	52,225	45,700	(19,000)	400	20,000		118,125	9.83
1911	32,775	81,210	(45,500)		15,750	500	130,235	10.36
1912	14,660	44,000	(32,423)	1,550	35,500		111,620	10.66
1913	2,903	44,175	(20,000)		26,000		73,078	4.97
1914	94,429	119,600	(67,500)		12,300		226,320	17.06
1915	6,610	21,000	(21,000)				27,110	1.6
1916	600	40,200	(40,000)				40,800	2.37
1917	10,000	46,000	(25,000)				56,000	2.98
1918		30,000	(29,000)				30,000	1.56
1919		71,500	(59,000)				71,500	4.48

Abstracted from Contract Registers, 1896–1919.
[1] Ten months only.
[2] Export Contracts.

death John Lang had become a man of some substance. Since 1900 he had drawn £11,937 from the partnership. (See Table 4.5 on page 36.) His estate was valued at £5,486, including £2,669 owing to him from Peter MacCallum & Sons, and £2,110 invested in ships. (See page 47.) He had also followed the fashion after the Boer War in buying £211 worth of stock in South African and Rhodesian mining companies.[26] The difference between the value of his estate and his drawings from Peter MacCallums alone between 1900 and 1903, apart from his earnings from Lang & Fulton, shows that he had wisely transferred capital to his children before his death to reduce his liability for death duty introduced in 1894.

Apart from his activities in Peter MacCallum & Sons and its associated company, Lang & Fulton (see chapter 5), John Lang had a wide spread of other interests. When in 1898 William Russell, son of Joseph Russell (one of the founders of Russell & Co) gave up his interest in John Hastie & Co, steering gear manufacturers of Greenock, John Lang became a director of the limited company that took over the concern.[27] He was prominent in civic affairs in Greenock. In 1875 he was elected a member of the Town Council, resigning in 1879 probably because he feared bankruptcy which would have

Table 4.4 P MacCallum & Sons – Sales to major customers: 1896–1919

Date	Russell & Co	Laird & Co	Scotts Ship-building & Engineering Co	R. Duncan & Co	William Hamilton & Co	Anderson Rodger & Co	Workman Clark	Cammell Laird
1896	3,970	310	428	3,100				
1897	1,310	25	1,500	3,000				
1898	3,500	350	13,000	6,000				
1899	4,840		7,790	3,900				
1900		40		1,500				
1901		65	12,100	5,300				
1902	3,400		150					
1903	3,500	1,080	220	550		1,300		
1904					3,000	2,800		
1905	9,560		8,350		4,900			
1906	3,690		12,850	2,720	2,100	100		
1907		2,000	2,275		4,300		200	
1908	5,500	2,000	200	5,500	6,000		22,300	
1909	6,170		1,220	4,072	9,550		25,800	3,500
1910	3,650	50	1,550	50	13,400		32,250	4,700
1911	8,450	3,000	17,160	8,800	23,500	2,000	42,500	8,200
1912	20,500	9,050	2,000	5,250			29,000	12,200
1913	19,500						19,000	10,000
1914	21,000	5.050	1,800	3,000	45,370		55,600	16,600
1915	11,000			500			9,000	
1916	22,000		600	2,000	15,000			
1917[1]								
1918[1]								
1919	14,800						20,000	

[1] There is no data for 1917 and 1918 as steel supplies were controlled.

*Baillie John Lang as Treasurer (to the left of the Provost)
with other members of Greenock Town Council in the 1880s*

automatically disqualified him. He returned to the council in 1882, being appointed treasurer in 1884 and magistrate in 1885. He was a member of the newly established school board from 1876 to 1879. He also served as president of the Chamber of Commerce and chairman of the Greenock Provident Bank.

John Lang, an elder in St Paul's established church, was a deeply committed Christian, concerned to do all he could to help his fellow men. He was a director of the Greenock Infirmary and on the committees of Sir Gabriel Wood's Asylum for seamen and the Greenock Medical Aid Society. He was active in establishing the Greenock Working Boys and Girls Society and in 1875 the Sunday Morning Free Breakfast movement, often writing articles for the newspapers describing the scenes when the 'poorest of the poor' were given meals. In 1881 he helped set up a committee to organize United Evangelistic meetings and was instrumental in bringing the famous American evangelists, Moody and Sankey to the town. With Abram Lyle, founder of the well-known sugar firm, he was a leading member of the Greenock Total Abstinence Society being largely responsible for raising funds to build the

Temperance Institute in 1869. On his retirement from the presidency of the society in 1896, he was presented with an 'illuminated address enclosed in a handsome casket' to mark his jubilee as an abstainer.[28] At his funeral the minister of St Paul's commented:

> 'Whatever our friend did or did not accomplish, no one will deny his single-mindedness, his zeal for social welfare, his readiness to do all that was in his power to make men happier and better, and to turn their attention to their home duties, and to whatever would help them to walk before God with a perfect heart.'[29]

A year before the death of John Lang, the capital of the partnership had been reconstructed when Louis Vandalle Fulton (James Fulton's second son) became a partner. The capital was increased to £11,937, with John Lang and James Fulton holding 3/10ths each and Peter MacCallum Lang and Louis Vandalle Fulton 2/10ths each. After John Lang's death, the capital was reduced to £10,000, with Peter MacCallum Lang holding one-half and James Fulton and his son a quarter each.[30] The depression in the shipbuilding industry continued throughout 1904. From 1905 to 1907 output recovered, buoyed up by Government spending on the first dreadnought. Peter Mac-Callum & Sons' business reflected this trend. Purchases and sales of steel recovered slightly in 1904, but profits remained under pressure. During 1905 purchases almost trebled to 57,447 tons, of which all but 660 tons were bought from Scottish producers, representing about 4.5 per cent of their output. (See Table 4.3 on page 32.) Although purchases fell slightly in 1906 and 1907 they remained at a high level. Russells, Scotts, and Duncans were joined as leading customers by William Hamilton & Co of Port Glasgow, founded in 1890.[31] At the same time the company began to build up an export trade, particularly in Norway, where local shipbuilding was developing to meet the needs of a burgeoning shipping industry. During 1906 and 1907 they shipped 7,650 tons to customers there who included Thorvald Kahrs, Nylands Vaerksted, and Geige & Co.[32] Profits in 1906 and 1907 recovered strongly reaching £7,673 in 1907, representing nearly 12 per cent on the greatly augmented gross tangible assets of £64,886. (See Table 4.2 on page 31.)

As 1907 progressed there were signs that the boom was about to burst. For those who held substantial investments in industrial concerns there were other ominous portents. During 1906 the Liberals had won a landslide victory on a manifesto committing them to raising death duties and introducing super-tax to pay for an ambitious social security programme. Death duties could be avoided by transferring money to relatives at least one year before death and after the 1911 budget, at least five years. Partnerships were not convenient for effecting such transfers. As a result between 1906 and 1911 a great number of unlimited partnerships were converted into limited liability companies, the shares of which could readily be dispersed to the partners' relatives. Family shareholders were offered considerable protection by the Companies Act of 1907, which recognized private companies for the first time. It allowed the promoters of such concerns to restrict the right to transfer its shares. It limited the number of members to fifty, prohibited any invitation to the public to subscribe for any shares or debentures and did not require the directors to publish a balance sheet.

In the van of the fashion, Peter MacCallum & Sons became a private limited liability company in 1907, together with its associated shipowning concern of Lang & Fulton. By the dissolution of the partnership, its members had become wealthy men. Between 1900 and 1908 James Fulton had drawn £20,087 including his paid-up capital of £2,500, Peter MacCallum Lang £22,665, and Louis Vandalle Fulton £8,893. (See Table 4.5 below.)[33] The capital of Peter MacCallum & Sons Ltd was fixed at £25,000, divided into 2,500 shares of £10 each. The shareholders in the new company were James Fulton, with 625 shares, his sons, Louis Vandalle Fulton, with 624, and Charles

Table 4.5 *Partners' Drawings from Peter MacCallum & Sons 1900–8*

Date	John Lang	James Fulton	Peter MacCallum Lang	Louis Vandalle Fulton
1900	5,237	4,015	120	70
1901	3,108	773	947	540
1902	2,537	2,602	723	113
1903	1,055[2]	867	1,576	126
1904		726	1,302	126
1905		1,750	1,037	1,047
1906		864	2,579	
1907[1]		885	149	
1908		7,605	14,232	8,623
Total	11,937	20,087	22,665	8,893

[1] *Half year only.*
[2] *John Lang died in 1903.*
Abstracted from private ledger No. 6.

Gibson Fulton with one, Peter MacCallum Lang with 1,247, and his wife Margaret Carswell Vandalle Lang, with one, his mother Jeannie Lyle Lang with one, and his sister, Alice Jane Lang with one.[34]

In 1907 the Port Talbot steelworks, which had been built in 1901 and closed in 1903, was revived and re-equipped by Colonel William Charles Wright on behalf of Baldwins Ltd and Gloucester Carriage Works. By using cheap continental ores and with a site close to the sea Wright reckoned to produce ship steel at cheaper prices than most other British plants. In this expectation Workman Clark, the Belfast shipbuilders and Russell & Co took parcels of shares in the new venture. It was probably no coincidence that MacCallums started doing business with Workman Clark during 1907. This custom resulted from the Lang's association with John Hastie & Co (Peter MacCallum Lang had succeeded his father as a director). Hastie purchased the bulk of their electric motors for driving their steering gear from Hugh J Scott & Co of Belfast which was owned by members of the Workman family.[35] MacCallums were attracted by Wright's offer of close collaboration as the prices he was quoting were about 10 per cent below those fixed by the Glasgow Iron Merchants Association.[36] This body had been formed in 1899 by the principal iron and steel merchants in Glasgow with the object of controlling prices and margins within a twenty mile radius of Glasgow. Peter MacCallum & Sons were not among the original members.[37] Indeed, they appear regularly to have done their best to undercut their competitors. Sometime later in 1907 MacCallums seem to have contracted to supply at least 20,000 tons of plate and angles a year to Workman Clark and to purchase at least 10,000 tons of angles from Port Talbot.[38] When the steel works was recommissioned it could only roll angles and it was not until 1909 that a new plate mill came into production.[39] So as to provide space for this

A heavy set of plate-bending rolls at Workman Clark's Belfast yard in about 1910, bending steel supplied by Mac-Callums from Port Talbot

enlarged operation, Peter MacCallum & Sons leased premises in 1907 (later purchased in 1913) at 1 Cathcart Street, Greenock, from Sir Andrew Noble and Benjamin Noble, directors of the armaments giant, Armstrong Whitworth & Co.[40]

During 1908, the first year of these new arrangements, MacCallums bought 10,000 tons of angles from Port Talbot and supplied Workman Clark with 22,300 tons of steel, more than they had ever supplied to a single customer in a year before. (See Table 4.4 on page 33.) They also pushed the level of their purchases in England to a record level of 22,964 tons, partly to cater for their established Norwegian customers and a new contract with the Taikoo Dockyard & Engineering Co of Hong Kong. They supplemented these by buying 3,000 tons of German steel from the great Thyssen Company and from Phoenix Hoerden.[41] This pattern of sales continued into 1909 with

MacCallums winning business from Cammell Laird & Co of Birkenhead which had its own steel works at Sheffield. During the year MacCallums opened a London branch following the closure of Pascoe Grenfell & Co in 1908. This secured custom from such well known companies as Finlay & Hodgson, London merchants; the Mount Stuart Dry Dock Co of Cardiff; Jessop & Co, London merchants; Armoured Tubular Flooring Co; Joseph Westwood & Co, structural engineers at Millwall; the London Graving Dock Co; and the Thames Iron Works Shipbuilding & Engineering Co.[42] The level of business achieved in 1908 and 1909 protected MacCallums from the slump in shipbuilding in these years and made the firm a powerful competitor for Scottish steel makers. Its purchase in 1908 and 1909 represented between 7 and 9 per cent of total Scottish ingot make. Although profits were only £4,139 in 1908, they recovered strongly to £8,761 in 1909. (See Table 4.6 below.)[43]

Table 4.6 *Capital and profits of Peter MacCallum & Sons Ltd, 1908–19*

	Profit £	Issued capital	Profit as % of capital
1908	4,139	25,000	16.5
1909	8,761	26,000	33.7
1910	10,426	26,000	40.1
1911	15,756	26,000	60.6
1912	17,988	26,000	69.2
1913	26,808	26,000	103.1
1914	26,998	26,000	103.8
1915	17,771	26,000	68.3
1016	20,350	26,000	78.3
1917	16,798	26,000	64.6
1918	21,017	250,000	8.4
1919	56,187	250,000	22.5

Abstracted from Minute Book No. 1 of Peter MacCallum & Sons Ltd, 1908–30.

One of the driving forces behind P MacCallum & Sons' sudden success in 1908 and 1909, seems to have been John D Dempster, who had joined the firm in 1899. In December 1909 he was appointed commercial director with 100 £10 shares. James Fulton, now aged sixty-one, retired from the firm and the share capital was reconstructed. The single shareholders remained as before. James Fulton junior took 550 shares, Louis Vandalle increased his stake to 699 shares, and Peter MacCallum Lang divided his holdings, retaining 812 shares himself and passing 435 shares to his brother, John James Lang.[44]

In 1908 Peter and Margaret Lang had their first son, Ian MacCallum, followed by another son James Fulton in 1909 and a daughter Dorothy in 1913. At the same time Louis Vandalle Fulton married Isabella Waterston, whose brother, Hugh, was to become managing director of Bairds and Scottish Steel Ltd. Their first son, James Vandalle, was born in 1909 and their second, Robert Waterston, in 1913.

Although the depression in the shipbuilding industry continued into 1910 P MacCallum & Sons Ltd again raised its trade. Purchases advanced to 118,125 tons, with 19,000 tons coming from Port Talbot and 20,000 tons being imported from Germany. MacCallums bought plates from Port Talbot and Germany at prices per ton of £5.75 and £6.00, whereas Scottish manufacturers supplied them for between £6.30 and £6.60.[45] During 1911 shipbuilding boomed. MacCallums purchased a staggering 130,235 tons of steel, drawing 45,500 tons from Port Talbot and a further 35,710 tons from other English manufacturers. Sales to Workman Clark jumped to 42,500 tons. The level of business declined in 1912 and fell sharply in 1913 as the boom peaked. (See Tables 4.3 and 4.4 on pages 32 and 33.) Nevertheless, profits continued to increase, rising from £10,426 in 1910 to £26,808 in 1913. (See Table 4.6 on page 38.) Despite a fall in sales, this growth is probably explained by an upturn in the stockholding side of the business during the boom and some customers paying for steel by long-dated bills. During 1913 the links between MacCallums, the Port Talbot Steel Co and its major customers, Russell & Co, and Workman Clark, were cemented by the formation of Ard Coasters Ltd to acquire three coasters to be employed carrying steel plates from South Wales to the Clyde and Belfast. (See page 62.)

Sales and purchases in the opening months of 1914 remained sluggish, but as the international situation became more tense during the summer they quickened as customers sought to secure supplies in the face of rapidly rising prices. After the declaration of war on 4 August 1914, they spiralled. By the end of the year MacCallums had purchased an almost unbelievable 226,320 tons of steel, equivalent to 17 per cent of the total Scottish ingot make. Of this 20,000 tons had been purchased from Port Talbot and 24,175 tons from English manufacturers. (See Table 4.2 on page 32.) Sales to Russell & Co, William Hamilton & Co, Workman Clark and Cammell Laird reached record levels of 21,000 tons, 4,537 tons, 55,600 tons and 16,600 tons respectively. (See Table 4.4 on page 33.) Profits reached a record £26,998. Directly hostilities commenced the Admiralty had powers to divert steel supplies for essential war work. With the formation of the Ministry of Munitions in June 1915 all steel production passed under Government control. Until the end of the year most shipbuilding capacity was diverted to warship building. Those yards like Russell & Co and Duncans who had specialized in tramp ships did not share in this work. During 1915 MacCallums' business slumped largely because their customers had stockpiled steel in the previous year. They purchased 27,110 tons of which 11,000 tons were sold to Russell & Co and 9,000 tons to Workman Clark. (See Table 4.4 on page 33.) Their London business and export trade dwindled to almost nothing. During 1916 their trade recovered to 40,800 tons, but it was well below the immediate pre-war level. This pattern continued until the termination of hostilities in 1918. During 1916 Peter MacCallum Lang was put in charge of organizing all steel supplies in the Clyde area – a highly important job which he discharged very efficiently until the end of the war. Family tradition has it that in the course of these duties he had occasion, in 1917, to attend a breakfast-time meeting with two future Prime Ministers – Stanley Baldwin of steel makers Baldwins Ltd, then Financial Secretary to the Treasury, and Winston Churchill, then Minister of Munitions in the wartime government. The meeting took place in the Adelphi Hotel, Liverpool and Churchill, disgruntled by a sleepless night on the train from London, declined to utter a word until he had first been brought, and had consumed, a large brandy and soda!

Following the mounting sinkings of allied tramp shipping by 'U'-boats in 1915 and 1916, a department of merchant shipbuilding was established early in 1917 in the newly formed Ministry of Shipping. It was directed from the start by James Lithgow who, with his brother Henry, had controlled Russell & Co since their father's death in 1908. He was assisted in this task by James Fulton. (See page 65.) James Lithgow quickly mobilized British merchant ship-building capacity, diverting for this purpose large supplies of steel from the recently greatly enlarged steel works.[45] One of the effects of this centralized control of merchant ship construction was that the shipbuilders became accustomed to deal direct with the steel makers rather than through merchants. At the same time, predicting an enormous boom in shipbuilding with the coming of peace, to replace vessels lost during the war, shipbuilders became anxious to secure their supplies of steel. Many opened negotiations to buy into steel works after the war.[46] Proposed mergers between shipbuilders and steel works boded ill for Peter MacCallum & Sons. In 1918 and 1919 they bought no steel at all from Scottish producers.

In looking ahead the directors of MacCallums could take comfort from their strong links with Port Talbot, Russell & Co and Workman Clark. The Port Talbot steelworks had been taken over formally by Baldwins in 1915 and expanded as part of the Government's programme to raise steel production.[47] Russells, which was renamed Lithgows Ltd in 1918, had acquired in 1912 the bankrupt business of Anderson Rodger and took over in 1915 Robert Duncan & Co, and in 1919 Dunlop Bremner & Co and William Hamilton & Co, all in Port Glasgow.[48] In 1916 Russells had come to an agreement with MacCallums to supply them at the end of the war with 1,000 tons of steel a week from Port Talbot for the first six months and 2,000 tons a week for the next six months.[49] In confirmation of these links, Peter MacCallum & Sons' subscribed capital was raised during 1918 from £26,000 to the authorized amount of £250,000. The Lang and Fulton families continued to own the bulk of the shares, but, partly as a result of the merger of Ard Coasters Ltd with MacCallums (see page 66), the Kingston Investment Co (a subsidiary of Lithgows Ltd, established in 1909) took 2,500 £10 shares, Workman Clark & Co 1,250 £10 shares and Colonel William Charles Wright, managing director of the Port Talbot steelworks, 1,250 £10 shares.[50]

The history of steel has too often been written from the standpoint of the producer rather than the merchant or the customers. The development of

MacCallums between 1877 and 1919 demonstrates the importance of the steel merchants in shaping patterns of demand and production. From 1879 Peter MacCallums & Sons recovered from being almost bankrupt to becoming one of the most important steel merchanting businesses in Britain. The firm's linkage with Port Talbot and the directors' determination to buy steel for their customers at as low a rate as possible in world markets presented a challenge to Scottish manufacturers.

East Indian

Chapter 5

Sail Away: Steam Back: Lang & Fulton 1876–1922

With the ending of John Elder & Co's patent over the compound engine in 1869 and the opening of the Suez Canal in the same year, the possibilities for using steam ships to carry cargo were greatly enhanced. From 1870 Thomas Turnbull & Sons of Whitby whose vessels traded principally to Baltic Ports, began to switch from sail to steam. By the end of the decade they had sold all but one of their sailing ships.[1] The new steamers were only profitable for carrying goods where margins were high. Some ship owners chose to build large sailing ships of between 1,500 and 1,800 tons, which, although much slower than steamships, were ideal for carrying bulk cargoes like coal and iron where margins were slim. These new investments caused a large number of second-hand vessels to come on to the market. Their low price attracted large numbers of businessmen in Britain's coastal towns and cities to enter the industry. There were advantages in owning ships as depreciation could be offset against income tax, re-introduced in 1846.[2]

At Greenock James and John Denholm established their well known shipowning business in 1872 when they bought the new 122-ton schooner, *David Sinclair*, built at Brixham. They extended over the next ten years by purchasing at least six second-hand ships.[3] John Lang and James Fulton followed this lead in 1876 when they acquired the *Lady Clarendon* of 1,331 tons in association with John and William Low, shipowners in Greenock. The following year John Lang joined William Rankin, another local ship-owner, in buying the *Eirene*.[4] The decision to invest in shipping, possibly, arose from Lang's knowledge of the industry acquired from his directorship of the Dumbarton Steamboat Co, which he had held since taking over his father's share in the firm at his majority in 1857.[5] Lang and Fulton must also

42

have been influenced by the common practice of Lower Clyde tradespeople, who supplied local shipyards and shipowners, themselves taking shares in tonnage so as to secure a tied market for their goods.

During 1878 John Lang confirmed his intention of diversifying into ship owning, when he was given permission to underwrite by the Glasgow Underwriters' Protection Committee.[6] Glasgow and Greenock have a long tradition of marine underwriting, dating back to 1744, when a group of merchants advertised that policies on ships and goods would be issued at the shop of Andrew Stalker, bookseller in Glasgow. In 1818 the Association of Underwriters and Insurance Brokers in Glasgow was instituted to regulate the West of Scotland insurance market.[7] The Association was remarkably successful, defeating attempts by insurance companies to capture their business. The Glasgow Marine Insurance Co (founded in 1839) and the Scottish Marine Insurance Co (established 1890) were short-lived. The Greenock Insurance Co, whose date of establishment is unrecorded, was wound up in 1867.[8] By the time John Lang became a member, risks insured by the Association were handled by some twenty broking firms, including William Euing & Co, Rose, Murison & Thomson and R. Russell & Co. These firms

James Fulton, partner in Lang & Fulton and Peter Mac-Callums & Sons, and the man responsible for the new shipping venture

either placed their business with their own syndicates, made up of individual underwriters, or with insurance brokers.[9] During the late nineteenth century, Glasgow syndicates had a large share of the British marine market, under-writing part of the Cunard fleet, the Clan Line, the Union-Castle Line, British India Line, the City Line, as well as hundreds of locally owned tramp vessels.[10] It is not known to which underwriting syndicates John Lang subscribed.

John Lang and James Fulton formed a new partnership under the name of Lang & Fulton to manage their shipping interest. Although this firm shared offices with Peter MacCallum & Sons, it was operated separately. Nothing is known about the careers of the *Lady Clarendon* or the *Eirene* under the management of Lang & Fulton. It is probable that they sailed across the Atlantic to Canada in the timber trade. Further acquisitions were delayed by the financial problems of Peter MacCallum & Sons and James Lang's trustees in 1878 and 1879. When these began to resolve themselves in 1880, the partners, encouraged by a slight upturn in the freight rates, bought the *Alexandra* from A C Robbins of Yarmouth, Nova Scotia.[11] This 915-ton wooden barque had been constructed in 1863 at Pleasant Cove in Nova Scotia. Lang & Fulton employed her to import timber from North America, almost certainly taking coal as the outward cargo. In 1883 the partners had their first taste of misfortune when the *Alexandra* was wrecked. Throughout the nineteenth century sailing ship operation was notoriously dangerous. There were regular reports in the press of sightings of sinking or foundering vessels.[12] Between 1845 and 1872 the 'Diamond K' fleet of Greenock operated by John Kerr and Abram Lyle lost twenty-nine of its seventy-five ships.[13]

The *Alexandra* was not replaced immediately. During 1884 the economy turned down sharply and freight rates collapsed dramatically since in the previous three years too many shipowners had invested either in steamships or large sailing ships, incorporating many novel labour-saving devices – particularly steam donkey engines for hoisting sails, raising anchors and working pumps.[14] The depression continued until 1887. During 1886 Lang & Fulton purchased the 912-ton iron barque *Mary Low* from John Low of Greenock, their partner in the *Lady Clarendon*. This vessel, renamed *East Anglian*, had been built for Low in 1876 by Robert Duncan & Co of Port Glasgow, as a replacement for the *Lady Clarendon*. She carried a crew of between fourteen and nineteen. In 1890 the crew comprised seven Scots, including the master and the mate, six West Indians and six Americans.[15] Like other tramp operators, Lang & Fulton traded her world wide in search of cargoes. As communications were difficult, the master would have borne much of the responsibility for securing freights at favourable rates and arranging itineraries. During 1890 she sailed from Queenstown to Liverpool and thence to Newcastle, New South Wales.[16] Lang & Fulton probably reaped good returns from the *East Anglian*, as the economy turned up in 1887 and remained buoyant until early 1890.

The iron barque Mary Low *later* East Anglian *painted with the Ailsa Craig in the background, in the 1870s*

In 1890 a severe recession set in with two Greenock shipyards failing and one stopping payment, which must have strained the new steel business of Peter MacCallum & Sons. It was not until the autumn of 1893, when the shipping industry had begun to recover, that Lang & Fulton acquired further tonnage. They were now sufficiently confident in their skills as ship managers and had amassed sufficient funds from their metal business to order two 1,700-ton steel barques from Robert Duncan & Co of Port Glasgow – one of Peter MacCallum & Sons' chief customers. (See page 33.) These two ships, named *East Indian* and *East African*, were delivered in 1894 and 1895.[17] Unlike their predecessors they were not owned by the partners, but by two limited liability companies, the Ship East Indian Co, and the Ship East African Co. Single ship companies had been formed since the 1860s to own steam ships which, because of their high cost, required a greater spread of shareholders who needed the protection of limited liability. They had the added advantage of facilitating access to mortgage finance and of safeguarding a fleet against a heavy loss on one of its components. As sailing ships became more sophisticated in the late 1880s and their cost rose, this form of owner-ship became typical for all tramp ships.[18] Before the introduction of death duties in 1894, there were drawbacks for families which owned ships in adopting limited liability status as depreciation and loss could not be written off against income derived from other sources. However, with the imposition of death duties there were powerful reasons for opting for limited liability status. As duty was not payable on capital transferred to relatives more than

45

The steel barque East African, *built by Robert Duncan &
Co for Lang & Fulton in 1895 seen here rerigged as a ship.*

one year before death, it represented a convenient way of distributing funds
around a family. Moreover, the donor often continued to control his capital
since most single ship companies had only a few voting shares, usually held
by the managers.[19]

The issued capital of the Ship East Indian Co and the Ship East African
Co was £1,300 divided into thirteen £100 shares of which £50 was to be
paid-up. In the case of the *East African* five members of the Lang family took
20 shares and seven members of the Fulton family 22 shares. The ship's
master, William Putt from Brixham and a relative took 10 shares and Peter
MacCallum & Sons' accountant, Robert MacPherson, 4 shares. The ship's
builders, Robert Duncan & Co, invested in 26 shares, Alexander Gray,
sailcloth makers in Glasgow, who had supplied the sails, 6 shares, and John
Niven of Port Glasgow, who had rigged it, 4 shares. Howard Houlder & Co,
shipbrokers of Glasgow, Liverpool and London, and associates of the shipping company, Houlder Brothers, subscribed for 20 shares. The remaining
shares were taken up by local people in Greenock and Glasgow. For example,
4 shares were taken by two members of the MacOnie family, engineers in

Table 5.1 Analysis of shareholdings in Lang & Fulton's Sailing Ship Companies: 1894–1903

Name	Occupation	Place	East Africa £50 shares	East India £100 shares	Australian £100	½ share of Grenada £100	Edenware £100	Ormsary £100
Andrew, William S	Schoolmaster	Bowness					2	
Birkmyre, James	Merchant	Port Glasgow					10	
Birkmyre, John	Ropemaker	Port Glasgow		10				
Bloke, Matthew	Engineer	Greenock		5				
Coath family	Shipmaster	Polpero		5				5
Colville, Archibald	Steelmaker	Motherwell				2		2
Craig, Thomas	Manufacturer	Gourock			6			
Davie, Robert	Timber merchant	Greenock		3	2			
Decent, Samuel Wheton	Shipmaster	Brixham				10		
Denholm, John	Shipbroker	Greenock	1	4				
Duncan, Robert & Co	Shipbuilders	Port Glasgow	26	20				
Elston, James J	Mariner	Topsham (Devon)						5
Ferguson, Robert & Co	Sailmakers	Greenock					6	5
Ferguson, Thomasina	Spinster	Greenock		3				
Fulton family		Greenock	22	41	27	20	40	24
Galbraith, John	Baker	Greenock				2		
Gebbie, Mrs Jessie C H	Widow	Greenock						
Gray, Alexander	Sailcloth maker	Glasgow	6					
Hamilton, Agnes	Widow	Glasgow						
Houlder, Howard & Co	Shipbrokers	Glasgow and London	20					
Joliff, Charles	Shipmaster	Polperro			10			
Lang family		Greenock	20	37	20	20	28	24
Lithgow, William Todd	Shipbuilder	Greenock			50			40
McBride, Peter	Cement maker	Port Glasgow	4					
McCulloch, Colin	Town Clerk	Greenock				2	2	
MacOnie family	Engineers	Greenock	4		6	14	20	40
MacPherson family	Accountants	Greenock	4	4	8	8	8	14
MacSymon's Stores Ltd	Chandlers	Greenock			6			
Mitchell, Mrs Eliza		Glasgow	3	2				
Moore, Robert & Co	Merchants	Glasgow						10
Murray, Helen	Spinster	Greenock						2
Nicol family	Coal merchants	Greenock	4		4			8
Niven, John	Rigger	Port Glasgow	4					
Orr, William	Retired shipmaster	Greenock						
Porter family		Glasgow					4	
Port Glasgow & Newark Sailcloth Co	Sailcloth makers	Port Glasgow			6		8	10
Putt family	Shipmasters	Brixham	10	2				
Ramsay, Gilbert Andrew	Joiner and Builder	Greenock		1				2
Reid, William	Minister	Malahide						1
Robb, Moore & Co	Merchants	Glasgow						
Ross, Robert A	Warehouseman	Glasgow					8	1
Skinner, Thomas & Co	Shipbrokers	Glasgow			10			
Thomson, John	Boilermaker	Greenock		2				
Vandalle family		Greenock		6	5			8
			£6,500: 130	£14,500: 145	£16,000: 160	£8,000: 80	£14,000: 140	£20,000: 100

Greenock, who were supplied by Peter MacCallum & Sons (see Table 5.1 on this page).[20]

The capital structure of Ship East Indian Co was similar with half the value of the shares paid up and Robert Duncan & Co holding 20 shares, John Denholm 4 shares, John Birkmyre of the Gourock Ropework Company which supplied the sails, 10 shares, and Thomas Coath, the master from Polperro in Cornwall, 5 shares.[21] It was prudent and so a common practice for managers to require masters to take shares in the vessels they skippered. Before the general introduction of radio communications around the turn of the century, the master was responsible for the conduct of the vessels for long periods and often had to fix cargoes for the owners. He only received instructions from the managers at lengthy intervals from the various Lloyd's stations around the world. It was well known in the industry that masters regarded the No 1 'tween decks as their own preserve, in which they could ship cargoes on their own behalf. By insisting that masters subscribed for shares, the managers reduced the risk of the vessel being traded for the master's, rather than the owner's advantage.

The issued capital of both companies was matched by overdrafts from the Clydesdale Bank of £6,500 each, secured as a charge over the vessels. The bank insisted that the vessels should be insured for their full value. Bank finance for shipowning seems to have have become common in the late nineteenth century. Although George Rae in his celebrated book, *The Country Banker*, cautioned branch managers about the dangers attendant in making advances against ships as collateral, his own bank, the North and South Wales Bank, made regular advances to shipowners. In April 1890, for example, an overdraft was allowed to P Iredale & Co, shipowners, to 'enable them to pay the deposit on a new steel sailing ship'. The most frequent form of security taken by the North and South Wales Bank was a mortgage over the vessel, taking either 64ths or shares as security. For instance, in October 1890, Thomas Williams & Co, shipowners of Liverpool, lodged 16/64ths of the *Miltaides* in exchange for 8/64ths of the *Cambrian Chieftain*.[22]

Both the *East African* and *East Indian* were to be managed by Lang & Fulton, which continued as a partnership. Operating records only survive for the *East African*. From her delivery in February 1895 she began trading world-wide following much the same pattern as the *East Anglian*. She left Port Glasgow with a cargo of coal for Rio-de-Janeiro, sailing from there to Newcastle in New South Wales, thence to San Francisco, and returning to Antwerp in June 1896. This voyage yielded a profit of £1,873. (See Table 5.2 on page 49.) The shareholders received a dividend of 10 per cent on their paid-up capital and £1,200 was transferred to reserves.[23] The *East Indian* probably completed a similar voyage with an equal return.

During 1895 the economy was badly depressed. Clyde shipbuilding was severely affected with, for example, Russell & Co making profits of less than 1 per cent on its capital compared with a normal return of over 20 per cent. William Todd Lithgow, sole proprietor of the firm since 1892, was accustomed to win contracts during hard times by offering to take shares in vessels. Between 1878 and 1908 he invested in no less than 176 ships built by the company.[24] In 1893 he proposed to Lang & Fulton that as a speculation they should order a new 2,000-ton ship to be built more or less at cost.[25] Lithgow was well known to John Lang and James Fulton as he was a major customer of Peter MacCallum & Sons. The proposal was adopted with the agreement that MacCallums would supply the steel. At the same time a similar arrangement was made with Robert Duncan & Co to build an equivalent vessel, the *Deccan*. She was sold at a profit before launching.[26] The Russell vessel, a fully rigged ship of 2,100 tons named *Australian*, was delivered in January 1897. Incorporating many labour-saving devices, she was one of the largest full-riggers registered at a Clyde port at the time. The capital was divided into 160 shares of £100 each, of which only £50 was paid, the balance being made up by a mortgage to the Clydesdale Bank. The pattern of shareholding followed that of the Ship East African Co with the Lang family holding 20

Table 5.2 Returns from Sailing Ship Companies: 1896–1910

Date	Company: Capital:	Ship East African Co £13,000		Ship Australian Co £16,000		Eastern Shipping Co ½ share of Grenada £8,000	
		Profit £	Profit as % of capital	Profit £	Profit as % of capital	Profit £	Profit as % of capital
1896		1,873	14.4				
1897		0	0				
1898		0	0	1,459	9.1		
1899		2,683	20.6	1,807	11.3		
1900		0	0	2,535	15.8	2,032	25.4
1901		1,958	15.1	0	0	0	0
1902		2,457	18.9	3,010	18.8	2,363	29.5
1903		0	0	0	0	0	0
1904		0	0	0	0	483	6.0
1905		−635	−4.9	605	3.8	0	0
1906		316	2.4	516	3.2	301	3.8
1907		970	7.5	925	5.8	0	0
1908		789	6.0			340	4.25
1909		−602	−4.6			0	0
1910		234	1.8			−1,081	−13.5
Sale price		4,000				7,200	
Average percentage annual return			5.15		6.78		5.0
Total income		10,043		10,587		4,438	
Capital gain		1,043				3,638	

shares, the Fultons 26, and Lithgow 50. The master of the ship Charles Joliff of Polperro in Cornwall, owned ten shares and the Port Glasgow and Newark Sailcloth Co, which supplied the sails, six shares. The remaining shares were distributed between Glasgow and Greenock people, with the Nicol and MacOnie families again subscribing.[27] On delivery of the *Australian*, the *East Anglian* was sold to Norwegian owners, who were building up their business using cheap second-hand tonnage.

Between 1897 and 1901 the economy boomed and freight rates advanced, buoyed up by the Boer War. Many tramp shipowners chose to abandon sail in favour of steam. For example, in 1898 Russell & Co switched to building steam ships. Consequently a large number of sailing vessels came on to the market, which could still be operated profitably in the long haul trades, especially to Australia and the west coast of South Africa. In 1897 Lang & Fulton accepted the management of the *Dechmont*, owned by the Dechmont Ship Co in which W T Lithgow was the largest single shareholder. This fully rigged steel ship of 1,700 tons had been constructed by Russell & Co in 1891. The Lang and Fulton families acquired a stake of 50 shares in the company. The rest of the 350 £50 shares were widely distributed amongst individuals from Birmingham to Aberfeldy.[28] During 1899 the partners purchased from Peter Denniston & Co of Greenock, a half stake in the steel four-masted barque, *Grenada*, which had been built in 1894, also by Russell & Co. The Eastern Shipping Co was formed to own their holding in the vessel, with the Lang and Fulton families subscribing a controlling interest. The remaining shares were allotted to people in Greenock and Glasgow. (See Table 5.1 on page 47.) Its capital, like its predecessors, was divided into £100 shares of which £50 was paid up, the remaining shares being made up by mortgaging the ship for half the value of the firm's holding to the Clydesdale Bank.[29]

The *Australian* in its first four years of service was employed in making three voyages round Cape Horn to San Francisco and back, carrying coals on the outward journey. She earned total profits of £5,803. (See Table 5.2 on page 49.)[30] The *East African* continued in the Australian trade, making a voyage which started in the summer of 1897 from New York to Sydney, thence to Newcastle (New South Wales), thence to Mollendo in Peru, on to Caleta Buena in Chile to load with nitrates and back to London in April 1899. During the trip the ship rounded Cape Horn twice and travelled over 10,000 miles. She made a profit of nearly £2,700.[31] During 1900 with the escalation of the Boer War, large quantities of supplies had to be shipped to South Africa by the Government in British vessels. Freight rates were driven up and nearly all British shipowners shared in the trade. During 1900 the *East African*, the *Australian* and the *Grenada* all carried cargoes of coals to Cape Town. The *East African* and the *Australian* then went on to Australia, returning to Europe via the west coast of America, earning profits of £1,958 and £3,010.[32]

The high freights at the turn of the century, encouraged many tramp shipowners to order new steamers of about 4,000 tons. As a result great numbers of relatively new steel sailing ships came onto the market at low prices. Lang & Fulton seized this opportunity during 1900 to take over the management of the *Arana* and *Valkyrie* (both 2,200 tons) from J D Clink & Co, a well known Greenock shipping firm of the period. These vessels had been built by Charles Connell & Co of Scotstoun, Glasgow, in 1891 and 1892. They proved unlucky investments for the partners. Both sank on their first voyages, the *Arana* on passage from Santa Rosalia in Mexico in 1900 and the *Valkyrie* in the River Elbe.[33] Undeterred the partners purchased the *Edenballymore* (renamed *Edenmore*) from Thomson Dickie & Co of Glasgow, owners of the Maiden City Line. This vessel, which was of about 3,000 tons, had been built in 1890/1 by Russell & Co. The *Edenmore* was placed in the

Two views of the ship Edenballymore *in a floating dock, probably being inspected with a view to purchase in 1901*

ownership of the Ship Edenmore Co, which had a similar capital structure to its predecessors with James Birkmyre (brother of John) of the Gourock Ropework Co and Archibald Colville of David Colville & Sons, the steel makers, being represented among the stockholders. (See Table 5.1 on page 47.)[34]

During 1902 freight rates collapsed and an estimated 80 per cent of British shipping became unprofitable. The depression lasted for almost a decade. In the crisis years of 1907–08 rates were on the floor at their lowest level for one hundred years and one million gross tons of British shipping was laid up. Many shipowners who had invested in steamers at the height of the boom were forced out of business. Those who had held on to their sailing ships lost their nerve, cut their losses and sold up. Others held on in the hope that better times were round the corner, reducing their costs by employing foreign crews, spending little on maintenance and sending their vessels on longer and longer voyages (sometimes of over three years' duration) in search of remunerative cargoes, particularly to the Pacific. The problems of British owners were added to by the French Government which established a system of subsidies and bounties to aid its domestic tramp industry. By 1906 it was clear that the days of sail were over. In 1910 Lloyd's of London, concerned about the very high risk of loss of sailing vessels as compared with steamers, increased insurance rates sharply, making it almost impossible for British owners to employ sail in the deep sea trade.[35]

Lang & Fulton were hit by the sudden onset of the depression in 1902. The *Grenada* earned profits of only £482 in its second voyage to Australia via South Africa from October 1902 to May 1904.[36] The *East African* and the *Australian* were dispatched in 1902 on long voyages which lasted about two years. The *East African* sailed from South Shields on the Tyne in October 1902, thence to Newcastle, Cape Town, across the Atlantic to Buenos Aires, round Cape Horn to Brisbane, on to Newcastle (New South Wales), on to Portland (Ontario), returning via Cape Horn with a cargo of wheat to Dublin in January 1905.[37] The *Australian* left Penarth laden with coal in April 1902 for Cape Town, across the Pacific to Tacoma in Washington State in ballast, to Melbourne, on to Newcastle (New South Wales), thence to Acapulco in Mexico, back to Newcastle, on to Turia and Iquique in Chile and home with nitrates to Dunkirk in France in April 1905.[38] These long trips resulted in a loss of £635 for the *East African* and a very small profit of £605 for the *Australian*.[39] In reporting these results the managers complained of the very low freight rates and the habit of 'French owners of bounty-fed ships ... simply throwing their vessels on the market, and accepting any rate offered'.[40]

Lang and Fulton were not despondent. During the summer of 1902 they agreed to order a 2,200 ton four masted barque from William Lithgow, whose order book was rapidly dwindling. Peter MacCallum & Sons, who were experiencing very low demand, were to supply the steel and Lithgow was to invest £2,000 in the ship.[41] Named the *Ormsary* after Lithgow's newly acquired Argyllshire estate, she was the last sailing vessel ever to be built by Russell & Co. She featured many labour-saving devices like brace winches and pumps for adjusting her trim.[42] The Ship Ormsary Co was formed to own her, with a capital of 200 £100 shares half paid, matched by the now customary mortgage from the Clydesdale Bank. The Lang and Fulton families subscribed 48 shares, Lithgow 40 shares, the MacOnie family 40 shares and the Port Glasgow and Newark Sailcloth Co 10 shares; Robert Ferguson & Co (sailmakers in Port Glasgow) 5 shares and Archibald Colville 2 shares (See Table 5.1 on page 47.) The *Ormsary* was delivered in January 1903 and dispatched to the Pacific.[43] While she was being constructed the partners took over the management of the 1,964-ton fully rigged ship *Kynance* from Gordon Cowan of Greenock for use in the nitrate trade.[44] She was joined late in 1904 by the *Thistle* previously managed by J D Clink. The *Thistle* was wrecked on her first voyage for the partners on Palmerston Island, Port Pirie, Portland, Oregon in November 1905.[45]

After John Lang died in October 1903, James Fulton had to divide his time between the shipping business and helping Peter MacCallum Lang and

The steel ship Kynance *was built for a single-ship company managed by C G Cowan & Co in 1895 by Anderson Rodger & Co, Port Glasgow, and acquired by Lang & Fulton in 1903*

his second son, Louis Vandalle Fulton, with Peter MacCallum & Sons. The management of Lang & Fulton devoloved on James Fulton, his eldest son, and John James Lang, John Lang's second son. They were keen to follow the fashion by acquiring a steamship. In the summer of 1904, William Todd Lithgow offered to build them a 4,000-ton steamer for £42,000, which, in 1900/1, would have cost £65,000. He was willing to arrange a mortgage for 50 per cent of the price to run for three years and to invest £2,500 in the venture.[46] The partners confirmed the contract, with Peter MacCallum & Sons supplying the steel.[47]

As the cost of the ship was much greater than any of those previously owned by Lang & Fulton, the partners began the tedious task of enlisting subscribers for their new venture. They approached all the shareholders in their previous companies, concerns they had contracts with in Australia, their shipping agents in Britain, and other individuals they knew to be interested in shipping stock.[48] They agreed with Lithgow that they would stipulate subcontractors who were prepared to take part of the risk:

> 'We are desirous of bringing in shareholders from your subcontractors who supply engineers and shipbuilders outfit, also wire rigging etc, windlass winches, ropes, steering gear, canvas, forgings, compasses etc, perhaps you will be good enough to give such a preference on being named by us.'[49]

Sometimes they offered contracts for repairs, coaling, victualling, and brokerage in exchange for investment. On 1 November 1905 James Fulton wrote to Charles D Toosey, a well-known Liverpool shipbroker:

> 'Regarding foreign coaling contracts. As advised we are offered £1,000. Not knowing you and something of your principals I am prepared to give you the refusal of this offer for prompt reply. You might get in touch with your friends regarding this.'[50]

It took the partners nearly three months and over a hundred letters to raise the necessary support from thirty-three shareholders, who included Robert Donaldson of the Clyde Iron Works, members of the MacOnie family, Emilie, wife of the master Captain Putt of Brixham, the Port Glasgow and Newark Sailcloth Co, and David Rankin, a sugar refiner in Greenock. (See Table 5.3(b) on page 55.)[51] They were fortunate in securing a charter for the ship before delivery for a maiden voyage to New York and on to Australia for £8,655 which it was estimated would yield a profit of nearly £2,000.[52] The ship, named *Ardgowan*, entered service on New Year's Day 1906 – the

Table 5.3 *Analysis of shareholdings in Steamship Companies*

Name	Occupation	Place	Steam-ship Ardgoil Co	Steam-ship Ardgryfe Co	Steamship Ardgarroch Co	Steam-ship Ardgair Co	Ard Coasters Ltd	Steam-ship Ardgorm Co	Steam-ship Ardgarry Co	Ard Steamer Ltd
Allan, Alexander		Rutherglen	0	0	1	1	0	0	0	0
Auld, Mrs Helen J	Widow	Burntisland	0	6	0	0	0	2	0	0
Blackburn, James	Carter	Gourock	0	0	0	10	0	5	0	0
Caird, Arthur	Shipbuilder	Greenock	0	0	0	0	0	0	0	0
Fleming, Alice M	Spinster	Rutherglen	0	2	0	0	0	0	0	0
Fulton family		Greenock	8	13	13	22	3	18	13	750
Holloway, John	Shipbroker	Dublin	0	0	5	5	0	0	0	0
Humphreys, James		Port Talbot	0	0	0	3	0	0	0	0
Kincaid, John G	Engineer	Greenock	0	0	0	5	0	5	0	0
Lamb, Charles G.		London	0	0	0	4	0	0	0	0
Lang family		Greenock	2	2	2	2	2	2	2	800
Lang & Fulton	Ship managers	Greenock	56	102	101	95	105	121	56	0
Lithgow, James and Henry	Shipbuilders	Port Glasgow	100	25	35	0	50[1]	0	100	0
McComas, Samuel	Shipbroker	Dublin	0	2	0	5	0	0	0	20
McKinnon, James		Glasgow	0	3	4	4	0	4	0	0
MacLaren family		Motherwell	0	2	0	1	0	0	0	0
MacOnie family	Engineers	Greenock	0	5	1	4	0	4	5	0
MacPherson, Robert	Accountant	Greenock	3	3	3	3	0	5	3	0
MacSkinning, James		Bothwell	0	0	0	5	0	0	0	0
Mitchell, George A		Glasgow	0	3	0	0	0	0	0	0
Murray, David		Glasgow	0	2	0	0	0	0	0	0
Murray, Crawford		Glasgow	0	0	0	5	0	5	0	0
Nicol, Duncan	Coal merchant	Greenock	2	0	0	0	0	5	2	0
Phillipson, B A		Dublin	0	0	0	0	0	0	0	20
Port Glasgow and Newark Sailcloth Co		Port Glasgow	4	3	0	0	0	4	4	0
Port Talbot Steel Co	Steel manufacturers	Port Talbot	0	0	0	0	25	0	0	0
Rankin, Matthew	Engineer	Greenock	0	5	0	0	0	0	0	0
Robb, Moore & Co	Merchants	Glasgow	0	10	15	10	0	10	5	0
Tannahill, Frederick	Superintendent engineer L & F	Greenock	10	10	10	10	0	10	10	0
Taylor, Mary	Spinster	Greenock	0	10	0	3	0	0	0	0
Whyte, Robert	Wire ropemaker	Rutherglen	0	1	0	1	0	0	0	0
Workman Clark & Co	Shipbuilders	Belfast	0	0	0	0	25	0	0	0

[1] Per Kingston Investment Trust Co.

Table 5.3(b) Shareholders in Steamship Ardgowan Co. Ltd.

Allan, Alexander B., manufacturer, Clyde Works, Rutherglen	1
Chisholm, Sir Samuel, newspaper proprietor, Glasgow	2
Davidson, Alexander, Kirkcaldy	1
Donaldson, Robert M., coal master, Clyde Iron Works	5
Fulton family	29
Gill, William Nelson, engineer, Glasgow	2
Johnson & Son, W. R., shipbuilder, Larkhall	1
Jones, Gwladys, Port Talbot	1
Kevevar, Allan J., shipping broker, Glasgow	3
Lang family	29
Latta, Robert, tanner, Dumbarton	5
Lithgow, William Todd, shipbuilder, Port Glasgow	25
McCowan, Samuel H., merchant, Dumbarton	2
McIntyre, John D., insurance broker, Glasgow	2
MacOnie family, engineers, Greenock	15
Macpherson, Robert, accountant, Greenock	3
MacSkinning, Ellen W., Monklands	5
Neilson, William M., insurance official, Glasgow	2
Nicol, Duncan, coal merchant, Greenock	3
Polson, John, merchant, Glasgow	2
Port Glasgow & Newark Sailcloth Co.	4
Putt, Emilie, Brixton	4
Rankin, Daniel, refiner, Greenock	5
Reid, Nicholas M., merchant, Glasgow	5
Reid, William, clergyman, Malahide	4
Robb Moore & Co., Glasgow	10
Smith, Lizzie C., Uddingston	5
Tannahill, Frederick J. C., engineer superintendent L. F., Greenock	10
Waw, John, insurance broker, Glasgow	8
Whyte, Robert, manufacturer, Clyde Works	2

founder member of the Ard fleet of steamers. The new line was quickly nicknamed 'Ard Times' by Clyde seafarers.

By the end of 1905 Lang & Fulton, like other shipowners who had held on to sail, faced a serious dilemma. They could not sell their sailing vessels without suffering a major loss and all they could do was to continue hawking them around the Pacific in the hope of picking up cargoes at favourable rates 'on the spot'. On 6 December 1905 James Fulton, junior, poignantly summed up the problems of the industry in a letter to Captain Coath of the *Ormsary*:

'I have just written you very fully . . . on the deplorable position of your ship, which you will see is serious. We are really at a loss to know what to do next with her – at the different ports you have been at it has been the height of the seasons – yet your ship could not be fixed. We do not know what business is coming to – the only consolation if it is any, is that there are others worse off – Nitrate is now coming home by steam at 18/9 per ton, and nearly 15,000 tons of sailing ship tonnage unfixed available on the coast – Steamers are also into North Pacific coal and grain ports, and we hear today offering at little over ship rates homewards from Australia with grain – It looks almost as if steam would supersede sail very soon now on the long voyages, and even before the Panama Canal opens, which makes aspect all the more serious. We like some of our neighbours have been thinking seriously of selling our whole fleet as they come home, but unfortunately at present this can only be done at a heavy loss . . . It is steam that is killing the sailor.'[53]

The year 1906 brought the partners little comfort. The *Australian, Dechmont* and *East African* all recorded modest profits (see Table 5.2 on page 49). However, on 13 September the *Ormsary* foundered off Cape Horn with all hands. The shareholders made a loss, despite the insurance money, of 20 per cent in the £1.[54] On 30 November the *Ancona*, which had recently come under the management of Lang & Fulton, burnt out in the Bay of Biscay.[55]

During 1907 Lang & Fulton's ship management business was greatly extended when they accepted four ships previously managed by J D Hart, a local man who had died recently. These were *Amasana* (1,436 tons), *Samoena*

The steel four-masted barque Ormsary, *delivered to Lang & Fulton in 1903, the last sailing ship built by Russell & Co, with the house-flag flying from the main mast*

(1,962 tons), *Calluna* (1,400 tons), and *Zinita* (1,633 tons).[56] They had all been built for J D Clink by Charles Connell & Co between 1891 and 1892. They were each owned by independent single ship companies whose shareholders included Charles and William Connell, members of the Robinson family, timber merchants of Glasgow and members of the MacOnie family, engineers, Greenock. The Lang & Fulton families took no interest in these concerns.[57] The *Amasana* was wrecked in Australia immediately after the take-over. Results in 1907 were better and the partners were able to transfer sums to the single ship companies reserve accounts.[58] The new steamer *Ardgowan* showed a good return. This healthier position reflected the formation in 1907 of a freight union among British tramp owners to fix a floor for freight rates to which Lang & Fulton subscribed.[59] During the year, like Peter MacCallum & Sons, they converted the business into a private limited liability company, presumably for the same reasons. (See page 36.) The two

*Aboard a steam yacht about 1910 with Robert Waterston,
father of Hugh at the helm, Jame Fulton in the foreground
and P M Lang, and their wives*

families held all the share capital, transferring the bulk of their shares in the single ship companies to the new company.[60]

Profits remained level in the first few months of 1908, but by the middle of the year freights had plunged and the union collapsed. All the company's sailing vessels were trading in the red. Between May 1908 and November 1909 the *East African* made a loss of £600 on a trip from London to Australia.[61] On a long voyage lasting from May 1908 to June 1910 to Santa Rosalia in Oregon, the *Grenada* recorded a loss of over £1,000. For much of this time the vessel was laid up in the Puget Sound waiting a charter at union rates, and, eventually had to be sent to Australia to secure a homeward freight.[62] During 1908 Lang & Fulton were encouraged by the continuing profitability of the *Ardgowan* to accept a tempting offer to build a 4,300-ton steamship for £43,000 from James and Henry Lithgow who had just taken over as partners in Russell & Co following their father's death in June.[63] They were desperate for work, as their yard 'had been practically idle for some months'.[64] They agreed to invest £2,500 in the single ship company which was to own the steamer and to buy the iron and steel for the vessel from Peter MacCallum & Sons, the castings from G & J MacOnie, deck and engineroom outfit from A Macpherson & Co, the boiler tubes from Wilsons & Unions, and the canvas work from Ferguson & Co. In return for these contracts the owners of these companies were prepared to invest in the new company.[65] In March 1909 Russell & Co offered another vessel of the same type built 'on spec' to Lang & Fulton for about £40,000 with the additional bonus that they would invest £10,000 in the owning company.[66] This ship, *Ardgoil*, was delivered in July 1909 and its sister ship, *Ardgryfe*, in September. Half the capital of the two owning companies was subscribed, the balance being made up by the familiar mortgages to the Clydesdale Bank. The capital structure of the *Ardgryfe* marked a new departure with the management company Lang & Fulton holding at least half of the shares.[67] This was a common trend at the time.[68] John J Lang had no doubt that these two vessels were a sound investment when he wrote to Captain Jones, soliciting support:

> 'Candidly I don't believe such good bargains were ever got from ship builders before.... The Freight market during the last few months has been gradually creeping upwards and looks like continuing and there is now a fair margin of profit in current freights for steamers of this fine up-to-date type and size, so that when the little extra filip comes, such as a bumper crop or two, or a war scare, large profits should be made by these fine money earners.'[69]

When Lang & Fulton decided to buy two new steamers, they put the sailing ships they owned or managed on the market as they completed their voyages. During February 1909 the *Australian* was posted missing with all hands, while on passage to Sydney to load wheat and in October the *Edenmore* was wrecked on Stronsay in the Orkneys and the *Kynance* at Tocopilla. Although these vessels were all insured through the Glasgow Marine Underwriters Association and entered in the Clyde Sailing Ship Owners freight and demurrage protection clubs, indemnity and running down clubs and the Clyde Sailing Ship Small Damage Association, the insurance did not cover the whole value of the vessels. Only £11,880 was paid out on the *Australian* compared with a first cost of £15,138 which had not been written down. (See Table 5.2 on page 49.) During 1910 the *East Indian*, *Dechmont*, *Grenada*, *Samoena*, *Calluna* and *Zinita* were sold mostly to Norwegian owners who could still operate them to advantage.[70] Lang & Fulton's last sailing ship, the *East African*, was sold in 1911 for £4,000, compared with the purchase price of £13,000 in 1895. During her service from 1895 to 1910 she had earned profits

58

The SS Ardgryfe, *built in 1909 for Lang & Fulton by Russell & Co. A typical tramp steamer of the period*

of £8,083 which, when added to the final sale price, shows a capital gain of a little over £1,000.[71]

The passing of sail made seafaring a much safer occupation. Under sail there was a constant risk of foundering far from land with no hope of survival and of running aground on rocky shoals. Eight of the sailing ships owned by Lang & Fulton were lost. On every voyage some members of the crew of a sailing ship could expect to die either from illness, falling overboard, or plunging to the deck from the rigging. There were always discipline problems. The crews of most British tramp sailing ships were of mixed nationality.[72] Those of Lang & Fulton were no exception. When the *East African* sailed from Rotterdam to Acapulco in 1907 she carried a master, two mates, a steward, a cook, a carpenter and a sailmaker, twenty-four able seamen, and seven apprentices. The crew consisted of Scots, Swedes, Norwegian, Germans, Americans and West Indians. On arrival at Acapulco six of the Swedish members of the crew deserted. The master had them arrested and imprisoned. V Veila, an able seaman, was absent without leave, returning paralytically drunk. John Aulin, a Swede from the Sailors' Home in Rotterdam, died of fever. His pitifully few personal effects illustrate poignantly the rigours of seamen's lives. He owned two coats, one pair of dungaree trousers, two shirts, two singlets, one jersey, one blanket, two mufflers, one pillowcase, one handkerchief, one dungaree jerkin, one waistcoat, one belt, two caps, six pairs of socks, one pair of mitts, two pairs of boots, one pair of sea boots, two suits of oilskins, one chitty box, and one deal box. He was well off compared

Table 5.4 Returns from Steamship Companies: 1910-1919

Company: Capital:	Steamship Ardgoil Co £40,000		Steamship Ardgryfe Co £40,000		Steamship Ardgarroch Co £36,000		Steamship Ardgair Co £40,000	
Date	Profit £	Profit as % of capital	Profit £	Profit as % of capital	Profit £	Profit as % of capital	Profit £	Profit as % of capital
1910	4,431	11.1						
1911	4,122	10.3	8,776	21.9				
1912	12,861	32.1	13,262	33.1	11,048			
1913	14,249	35.6	18,410	46.0	18,818			
1914			11,117	27.8	7,722		7,206	18.0
1915			24,497	61.2	16,380		9,337	23.3
1916			26,488	66.2			52,565	131.4
1917			7,502	18.7	34,712		8,908	22.3
1918								
1919								
1920								
Sale Price	46,000		150,000		135,000		175,000	
Average percentage annual return		22.3		39.3				48.7
Total income	35,663		110,052				78,016	
Capital gain	41,663		220,052				213,016	

Company: Capital:	Ard Coasters Ltd £42,000		Steamship Ardgorm Co £40,000		Steamship Ardgarry Co £52,000		Ard Steamers Ltd £150,000	
Date	Profit £	Profit as % of capital	Profit £	Profit as % of capital	Profit £	Profit as % of capital	Profit £	Profit as % of capital
1910							11,991	8.0
1911							69,840	46.0
1912							9,000 (dividend only)	6.0
1913								
1914	2,842	6.8						
1915	12,050	28.7	4,713	11.8	18,179	34.9	28,115	18.7
1916	23,109	55.0	41,590	104.0	6,830	13.1	255,000	
1917	1,656	3.9	72,091	180.2	21,733	41.8		
1918					N.A.			
1919					N.A.			19.8
1920					N.A.			
Sale price	60,000		175,000		N.A.		118,946	
Average percentage annual return		23.6		98.7		29.9	223,946	
Total income	39,657		118,394		N.A.			
Capital gain	157,657		253,394		N.A.			

to others. One month out from Acapulco bound for Tacoma, John Smidt was washed overboard and drowned. All he owned was a jacket, a pair of trousers, a pair of drawers, a shirt, a pair of boots, two felt hats and the clothes he was drowned in.[73]

Lang & Fulton's investment in steamships proved highly profitable. Freight rates crept up through 1910 and 1911. By 1912 the worst of the depression was over and 1913 and 1914 were boom years – the high tide of British mercantile prosperity. In its first year of service ending in July 1910, the *Ardgoil* completed two round voyages, first from the Clyde to Pensacola in Mexico, on to Buenos Aires with timber, thence to Port Pirie in Australia and home with ore to Antwerp; second from Cardiff to Colombo with coals and home from Calcutta with a mixed cargo to Dunkirk and Hull. She earned a profit of £4,431.[74] The *Ardgryfe* completed two similar voyages between September 1909 and March 1911, yielding profits of £8,776.[75] (See Table 5.4 on page 60.) This spectacular success encouraged Lang & Fulton to order a 9,500-ton steamer from the Port Glasgow shipbuilders, William Hamilton & Co to be built on joint account as a speculation.[76] This vessel was sold at profit before delivery to the Isthian Steamship Co. Her position in the fleet was taken by the *Otterburn* renamed *Ardgarroch* of 8,500 tons (the same class as the *Ardgryfe*) built in 1907 for Robert Shankland & Co of Greenock by Russell & Co at a price of £44,000. She had been involved in a collision at Antwerp and Robert Shankland & Co found themselves unable to pay for the repair. Henry Lithgow, a shareholder in the ship, approached Lang & Fulton with an offer to invest £3,500 if they took the ship over. Lang & Fulton purchased the ship for £41,000 in November 1911 and assumed responsibility for meeting a repair bill of £3,700.[77]

The results for 1912 were even more spectacular than 1911, with *Ardgoil* making profits of nearly £13,000, the *Ardgryfe* nearly £10,500 and the

The SS Ardgair, *a bigger version of the* Ardgryfe, *built in 1913 by Robert Duncan & Co for a single-ship company managed by Lang & Fulton*

Ardgarroch £11,000 after only nine months service.[78] The typical voyages were outwards with coal and home with grain from America or Australia. Lang & Fulton immediately ordered two new 8,500-ton steamers from Robert Duncan & Co, the *Ardgair* and the *Ardgorm* for delivery in 1913 at a cost of £50,805 and £60,000 respectively. It was agreed that John G Kincaid, engineers of Greenock, would supply the engines and take a stake in the companies formed to own the vessels.[79] At the same time it was decided to form a new concern, Ard Coasters Ltd, to operate a small fleet of coastal vessels to be employed in transporting steel ship plates and angles from Port

The coaster Ardgour *built for the ship-steel trade by George Brown & Co of Greenock for Ard Coasters Ltd in 1913, and managed by Lang & Fulton*

Talbot to Belfast and the Clyde. Three 1,500-ton steamers, *Ardgarth*, *Ardglass*, and *Ardgour* were ordered from George Brown & Co of Greenock. Russell & Co, through its subsidiary, the Kingston Investment Co, took 50 £100 shares in the venture, the Port Talbot Steel Co, 25 shares, and Workman Clark & Co, 25 shares.[80] The structure of the shareholding in the three new companies formed in 1912 followed the pattern set by the Steamship Ardgryfe Co with the management company owning at least half the shares. Arthur Caird, a director of Caird & Co, the Greenock shipbuilding firm and a customer of MacCallums, subscribed for ten shares in the Steamship Ardgair Co.[81]

Profits continued to mount during the first half of 1913, but fell away later in the year as the peak of the boom passed. (See Table 5.4 on page 60.) By this time nearly half of British merchant tonnage had been built since 1905.[82] Competition was severe and all attempts to maintain a freight union among tramp owners abandoned. In April 1913, Lang & Fulton were able to cancel the mortgages to the Clydesdale Bank on the *Ardgowan*, *Ardgoil*, *Ardgryfe* and *Ardgarroch*.[83] During August 1913 the *Ardgoil* was sold on a falling market for £47,000 less £1,000 commission, a profit of about £6,000 on the first cost.[84] Early in 1914 Lang & Fulton bought for £52,000 the 7,900-ton *Ardgarry* from Russell & Co, which had been ordered as the *Loch-Na-Torran* by the Loch line and cancelled. The Lang and Fulton families owned all 200 £100 shares in the new company.[85]

Between 1910 and 1914 the Lang and Fulton families extended their insurance interests. Recognizing that there would not be openings for all the Fulton children in the steel and shipowning business, Charles Gibson Fulton (James Fulton's third son) had learned the trade of insurance broking, probably with the Glasgow firm of J D McIntyre & Sons. There were advantages for both the steel and shipowning companies in having a direct

Table 5.5 *Lang & Fulton – Profits and returns on Capital: 1909–17*
Capital: £20,000

Date	Profit £	Profit as % of capital
1909	3,234	16.17
1901	4,662	23.31
1911	6,900	34.5
1912	6,301	31.5
1913	17,156	85.78
1914	14,489	72.45
1915	37,897	189.48
1916	59,711	289.55
1917	30,218	151.09

connection with a brokerage concern, particularly at a time when the size and number of their risks was rising quickly. Nearly all the Glasgow insurance brokers that were members of the Underwriters' Association were closely linked by family ties with local shipping lines. For example, the brokers Patrick Henderson & Co, were associated with Paddy Henderson (the Far East shippers), the Anchor Line, and the Irrawaddy Flotilla Co. When J D McIntyre died in 1907, Charles Gibson Fulton became a partner and the firm's name changed to McIntyre & Fulton.[86] In 1910 he was admitted as a broker by the Association and in 1917 he was given permission to underwrite for the London & Provincial Marine & General Insurance Co, one of the most successful marine insurance companies.[87] During 1914 he formed an underwriting syndicate, presumably with the chief purpose of writing business for the two family firms. Its members were Peter MacCallum Lang (who was allowed to underwrite up to £150), John James Lang (to £150), Henry Lithgow (to £150), and Charles Gibson Fulton (to £100).[88]

At the outbreak of hostilities, demand for shipping expanded, freights rose, and ship owners prospered. A P Lyle, managing director of Lyle

Shipping Co, one of Lang & Fulton's competitors on the Clyde, commented: 'it was a boom, an unprecedented one. During the war large profits were earned and could not but be earned.'[89] Some shipowners did not reap these rewards as their vessels were requisitioned by the government which only paid a 'blue book rate' calculated on the basis of the low rates of 1914.[90] At first the only Lang & Fulton ship to be requisitioned was the *Ardgarry* which was taken over from the start of the war.[91] The rest of the fleet continued to trade world wide. The *Ardgarroch* was time chartered to Canadian Pacific Railway Co on the London–St John's (New Brunswick) run, earning over £20,000 in 1915. In the second year of the war the *Ardgair* earned profits of nearly £32,000.[92] From March 1915 to February 1916 the *Ardgorm*, while employed on a time charter in the North Atlantic trade, yielded profits of £41,590, two-thirds of its costs.[93] Lang & Fulton's profits were equally large, rising from £14,500 in 1914 to nearly £38,000 in 1915 and almost £60,000 in 1916.[94] (See Table 5.5 on page 63.) These high earnings reflected the greatly increased cost of replacing tonnage due to wartime wage inflation.

Late in 1914 Lang & Fulton contracted with William Hamilton & Co for two new 9,000-ton steamers and early in 1915 for a 10,000-ton vessel.[95] Since Hamiltons were engaged in essential war work delivery was delayed.[96] The fleet was depleted in April 1915 by the sale of its founder member, the *Ardgowan*, to the Westminster Shipping Co for £66,000 – £23,000 more than she had cost.[97] Lang & Fulton were now desperate for new tonnage. They turned to Russell & Co for help, placing orders for two 7,900-ton steamers during the autumn of 1915 on behalf of the Steamship Ardgarry Co at a cost of £73,000 and £80,000.[98] Russells, which was managed by Henry Lithgow in his brother's absence on war service, was chronically short of work as it had received no government contracts since it specialized in merchant work.[99] During 1916 with the mounting loss of merchant ships to the U-boat campaign, the Admiralty began to release supplies of steel for merchant shipbuilding. Russell & Co delivered the *Ardgrange* and the *Ardgask* at the end of the year.[100] In March 1916 the Ardgarry Co ordered two more vessels of the same type at a cost of £180,000, followed by an order for a further two in November at a cost of £195,000.[101] During 1915 Ard Coasters Ltd had also ordered two 1,100-ton coasters, *Ardgarvel* and *Ardgantock*, from Ferguson Bros of Port Glasgow, not delivered until January and December 1917.[102] The 10,000-ton steamer built by Hamiltons was completed in July 1917 and immediately sold.[103] She was torpedoed the following month. During 1917 the *Ardglamis* and *Ardgay* were completed by Russell & Co and the *Ardgoil II* by Hamiltons. The *Ardgoil II* was placed in the ownership of a new company, Ard Steamers Ltd, whose capital was subscribed entirely by the Lang and Fulton families (See Table 5.3, on page 54.) She was immediately requisitioned by the government.[104]

As this new tonnage entered service, the Ard Line's profits came under pressure as the majority of its vessels were requisitioned for war work and those that remained free had to submit to the discipline of the convoy system. Lang & Fulton's profits fell back to £30,218 in 1917.[105] Those for Ard Coasters Ltd retreated from £23,000 in 1916 to £656 in 1917. (See Table 5.4 on page 60.) The line was fortunate not to lose any ships through enemy action until 1917, the height of the unrestricted U-boat war. In March the *Ardglass* was captured by *U-65* and sunk with explosives. The crew were all saved. The following month *U-35* torpedoed the *Ardgask* off Cape Rosello, Sicily, with one loss of life. On 9 November, barely a month after entering service, the *Ardglamis* went down 125 miles off Cape Spartel with no loss of life, a victim of *U-63*. Later in the month the *Ardgorm* was sold to the Norfolk and North American Steam Shipping Co for £175,000 – £115,000 more than its first cost.[106]

The very high level of sinkings during 1917 forced the government to form a department of merchant shipbuilding headed by Col James Lithgow who was assisted by James Fulton junior. Merchant shipbuilding under their skilful management was rapidly accelerated, using a series of standard ships, until, by the peace, new deliveries were exceeding sinkings.[107] During 1918 Lang & Fulton took delivery from Russell & Co of the *Ardglass II*, the *Ardgorm II*, the *Ardgroom* (initially *Ardgask II*), and from William Hamilton & Co of the *Ardgowan II*. The first three joined the Steamship Ardgarry Co and the last Ard Steamers Ltd.[108] Four coasters of between 1,100 and 2,000 gross tons, *Ardgartan*, *Ardgirvan*, *Ardgryfe*, and *Ardgarroch* were received by Ard Coasters Ltd. All eight ships were requisitioned by the government. In financing all these additions, Lang & Fulton continued to rely on the well proven expedient of mortgaging them to the Clydesdale

One of the Lang & Fulton tramp steamers in the dazzle painting scheme devised by Muirhead Bone to combat the U-boat campaign of 1917

Bank. Ard Coasters Ltd was wound up in October 1918 and its business transferred to Peter MacCallum & Sons as part of the arrangements with Russell & Co (now Lithgows Ltd), Workman Clark & Co and the Port Talbot Steel Co which were to come into effect as the end of the war.[109] MacCallums took over the *Ardgarvel*, *Ardgryfe II*, and *Ardgarroch II* with contracts for two more vessels to be delivered in 1919. Before the coming of peace, Lang & Fulton lost two more vessels. The *Ardgantock* was run down by HMS *Tartar* and *Ardglass II* torpedoed by *U31* six miles off Larne, with the loss of six lives.[110] During 1918 the *War Fantail*, an 8,000-ton steamer newly built by Robert Duncan & Co for the Ministry of Shipping was placed under the management of Lang & Fulton and requisitioned for war work.[111]

With the return to peacetime trading, the outlook for British shipping was not rosy. During the war the British merchant fleet had been depleted by sinkings, while those of other countries, particularly Japan and the United States, had expanded. British owners had been forced to withdraw from some trades and areas, especially the Pacific, allowing foreign companies to win their business. In April 1919 Sir Owen Philipps, head of the mighty Royal Mail Shipping Group, declared: 'We may find it by no means easy fully to re-establish ourselves in our ordinary sphere of operations. . . . I fear the working men of this country will have to face a period of leanness and unemployment.'[112] The larger shipping concerns, like Royal Mail, Furness Withy and P & O who had borne the brunt of the losses, were in urgent need of new tonnage by 1918 so as to meet the challenge of foreign competition in the coming peace. All shipbuilding berths were booked up for several years ahead and the big companies looked to buy second-hand vessels to replenish their fleets in the meantime. Many small tramp shipowners, only too familiar with the uncertainties of peacetime trading, took advantage of this demand to sell up.[113] For example, Sir William Burrell, the Glasgow shipowner, sold the whole of his Strath fleet of steamers.

The Ard fleet was a rich prize. The bulk of the vessels had been built by Russell & Co not to standard war-time specifications, but to Henry Lithgow's own standard designs which were reckoned to be amongst the best.[114] During 1918 the directors of Lang & Fulton decided to sell its deep sea fleet as the vessels were released from government contract, preferring to concentrate their effort and capital on the original steel business for which the prospects appeared excellent. In the spring of 1918 the *Ardgryfe* and *Ardgarroch* were sold to Cayzer Irvine's Clan Line. During April 1919 the *Ardgarry*, *Ardgrange*, *Ardgay*, *Ardgorm* and *Ardgroom* were purchased by Furness Withy. Later in the year arrangements were made to dispose of the *Ardgoil II* to the Ben Line of Leith and the *Ardgowan* to the Silver Line of London. Some of the coasters were also sold, the *Ardgirvan* to the European Gas Co, and the *Ardgryfe II* and *Ardgarroch II* to Mead Son & Hussey of London. During April 1919 the coaster *Ardgartan* was lost on passage from Swansea to Brest with all hands. No records survive of how much these sales realized; it was probably in excess of £1,500,000. Lang & Fulton and all the single ship companies were wound up and their assets realized.

The story of Lang & Fulton's shipping venture from the 1870s until the end of the First World War is typical of many British tramp shipping concerns of the period. With their strong connection through Peter MacCallum & Sons with the Lower Clyde shipbuilding industry, the firm had been able to acquire tonnage cheaply during depressions by sharing their risks. The spectacular success of its investment in steamers after 1906 had made the members of the Lang and Fulton families and their shareholders people of substance. However, by the end of the war they had to make a choice between steel merchanting and shipowning. The high costs of new tonnage and its greater carrying capacity made it impossible to run a tramp shipping line as an ancillary to the main business.

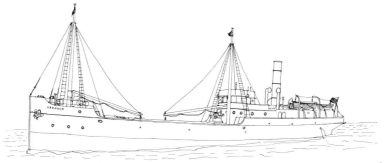

SS Ardgartan

Chapter 6

Steel through the Storm: 1919–1945

Indian Summer 1919–1929

At the coming of peace, it was difficult for steel merchants and stockholders to judge the future. The effect of the war on continental producers, particularly those in Germany and Belgium, was hard to assess, while at home many shipbuilders, who had become accustomed during the war to dealing directly with steel makers, appeared to be about to make these links formal through a series of mergers. In the very short term the outlook was good and steel merchants overlooked these long term problems in the scramble to return to peace time trading. During 1919 there was a massive boom in shipbuilding as owners sought to replace tonnage lost or worn out in the war.[1] This led to steel shortages which were due in part to a scarcity of ore in the United Kingdom resulting from the shortage of shipping as Government controls over it were only gradually relaxed.[2]

P. MacCallum & Sons would seem to have reaped the benefits of this boom. During 1919 they purchased 69,000 tons of plates and angles from Port Talbot and sold 9,000 tons of it to Lithgows and 20,000 tons to Workman Clark.[3] The firm became members of a syndicate with five other steel-merchants, including H H Skelton, one of the largest British merchants, and, Brown & Tawse of Dundee, to buy war surplus ship steel from the Ministry of Munitions.[4] In November 1919 MacCallums joined with Lithgows to purchase over the next year 16,221 tons of American ship plates for merchanting. At £16.50 a ton, this was, by May 1920, £10 cheaper than the price quoted on the spot in Scotland.[5] By April 1921 the partners had earned a profit of nearly £26,000 on an outlay of a little over £270,000.[6] These two ventures helped to swell MacCallums' profits in 1919 to a record

£56,187 (see Table 4.6 on page 38), of this £30,000 was used to create a reserve fund.[7]

By 1920 the prospects for steel merchants had become uncertain. In the first half of the year steel rose swiftly in price. The cost of ship plates in Scotland jumped from £21 in January to £26 by May.[8] Shipbuilders became determined to diversify into steel making in an effort to reduce costs and secure supplies[9]: during the year David Colville & Sons was acquired by Harland & Wolff, the Belfast and Glasgow shipbuilding concern, itself interwoven with the giant Royal Mail Shipping Group; the Glasgow Iron & Steel Co with its works at Wishaw was taken over by William Beardmore & Co and Swan Hunter & Wigham Richardson; and the Steel Company of Scotland by a consortium of Clyde shipbuilders. Of greater concern to MacCallums was Lithgows' purchase of James Dunlop & Company, proprietors of the Calderbank Steel Works, and Workman Clark's takeover of the Lanarkshire Steel Co.

James and Henry Lithgow's decision to buy James Dunlops was almost certainly a tactical move to ensure their group of yards would not be disadvantaged should local production costs (which had risen markedly during the war) fall below those of Baldwins and foreign suppliers. Otherwise they would not have lifted their shareholding in Baldwins by £12,000 to almost £55,000 in late 1919 when the capital was raised.[10] Workman Clark's investment in Lanarkshire was part of a much wider grouping put together in 1919 by Sir Edward Edgar, a London financier and company promoter, through Sperling Co, with help from members of the Workman family.[11] Between 1919 and 1921 in a series of complicated transactions the combine, known as the Northumberland Shipbuilding Group, came to embrace Workman Clark, Fairfields, the Monmouth Shipyard (built during the war), and the Northumberland shipyard at Howden on Tyne. The group also made an offer of £3 for each ordinary share of Baldwins which was accepted. However when Excess Profits Duty was raised from 40 to 60 per cent in the 1920 budget, the bid lapsed. The Workman family, while engaged in these important plans, did not overlook their long connection with MacCallums.

Immediately after Workman Clark became associated with the group, an agreement was signed with Baldwins (a component of the takeover deal) for the supply of steel at a fixed rebate on the market price to the Belfast yard using MacCallums to provide shipment.[12] As part of this arrangement 8,250 £1 shares in MacCallums were purchased by the Northumberland Shipbuilding Group, and, for reasons that can not now be discovered the directors of MacCallums were appointed 'managing directors for a ten year period'.[13] However, with the lapsing of the bid, the contract with Baldwins was broken and the 8,250 £1 shares were repurchased by members of the Lang and Fulton families in December 1920.[14] Workman Clark were unwilling to bind themselves to buying British steel when continental steel could be obtained for almost £3 per ton less than the prices quoted by Baldwins.

On 26 July 1921 William Strachan, managing director of Workman Clark wrote to Peter M Lang:

> 'We are of course very anxious to place our orders with our friends but . . . we are up against important shipowning clients drawing our attention to the fact that continental steel can be obtained now at £7. 10s. 0d f.o.b. Rotterdam . . . I am aware of course that the root cause of the steelmakers trouble is like our own and everybody else's inflated costs of production combined with diminished output . . .'[15]

In the absence of purchase and sales records it is hard to judge MacCallums' performance in 1920. The year resulted in a loss of £6,957; but Peter Lang, the chairman, suggested that this was due more to the payments of Excess Profits Duty for 1919 than to poor trading.[16] This may not have been the case. Early in the year the freight market had collapsed with rates retreating swiftly to their pre-war levels. At MacCallums, despite the delivery of *Ardglass* and *Ardgantock* at the beginning of the year, shipping income fell from about £41,000 to a little under £26,000. (See Table 6.2 on page 73.) At the annual general meeting John D Dempster's directorship was confirmed and Charles McKinlay Duncan (a senior employee) was appointed for the first time.

By the beginning of 1921 the economy was moving sharply into recession. During the year freight rates plummeted and orders for ships placed during the short lived boom were cancelled. This sudden downturn in demand was reflected in the collapse of the prices for ship plates and sections in Scotland from about £23 per ton in January to just £10 by the end of the year.[17] MacCallums do not seem to have been badly hit, probably because their principal customers Workman Clark and Russells were well occupied with contracts throughout the year. No sales or purchase records survive; but the company managed to record a small profit of £2,122 after the payment of Excess Profits Duty.[18] The shipping income rose to about £37,500. It is likely that in the prevailing conditions much of the fleet of seven coastal vessels was employed in carrying steel from Port Talbot to Belfast and the Clyde. As the outlook for shipping was bleak and prices of new tonnage was falling rapidly, the directors depreciated the book value of the fleet by £30,000 in 1920.[19] This sum was placed in a special ship replacement fund, which was invested in Government stock.

The improvement in the Company's shipping turnover in 1921 may also be explained by the revival of imports of steel from the continent. As early as May 1921 the National Federation of Iron and Steel Manufacturers were complaining to the Government of ruinous competition from Belgium, France, Luxemburg and Germany.[20] With the benefit of much lower wages, taxes and railway rates than in Britain, steel makers in these countries were able to quote prices far below their British competitors. The cheapness of foreign steel made many of the shipbuilders who had bought steel-making concerns in 1919 and 1920 reluctant to depend entirely on their tied suppliers.

It is unlikely that MacCallums, with their commitment to the import trade before the war, did not resume buying European steel at the earliest

Table 6.1 Contracts with suppliers of Merchant Steel, by origin of steel, 1922–39

Year	British make (tons)	Continental make (tons)	Total	Total sales
1922	14,050	28,200	42,250	49,535
1923	11,780	8,500	20,280	23,747
1924	13,680	59,380	72,960	64,351
1925	6,350	37,000	43,350	51,065
1926	26,588	58,125	84,713	102,257
1927	5,380	46,250	51,630	75,919
1928	46,550	16,260	62,810	70,187
1929	153,570[1]	18,500	172,070	133,367
1930	2,500	2,750	5,250	16,236
1931	0	0	0	5,025
1932	0	0	0	2,485
1933	200	0	200	23,450
1934	21,676	0	21,676	28,428
1935	47,768	0	47,767	35,645
1936	48,983	0	48,983	53,416
1937	8,025	0	8,025	8,192
1938	11,572	0	11,572	3,857
1939	7,960	0	7,960	8,600

[1] *Part of a contract for 3,400 tons was cancelled in 1931*
Source: *Abstract Contract Books 1911–65.*

opportunity. They had a fleet of seven modern coasters able to ship steel in 1,000 ton lots, offering a good blend of economy and convenience. During 1922, the first year after the war for which purchase figures survive, the company bought 42,250 tons of steel of which 28,200 tons came from Europe.[21] These first recorded post war continental purchases were drawn from established pre-war suppliers like Henschel & Sohn (5,000 tons), Gute-hoffnungshütte (1,000 tons), and new contractors like Mannesmannrohe Werke, Dusseldorf (8,500 tons). MacCallums also began buying through agents, which they had rarely done before, taking 15,000 tons of German steel through the Dundee firm of Brown & Tawse, and the London firm of R H Ferguson. Just over 12,000 tons of the British purchases came from firms that were connected with MacCallums through Workman Clark and Lithgows, 7,000 tons from Port Talbot, 3,000 tons from James Dunlop & Sons and 2,000 tons from Lanarkshire. The price quoted even by these tied suppliers was between £1 and £2 a ton higher than their continental competitors. Consequently even Workman Clark and Lithgows, despite their large investments in the British steel industry, purchased German steel through MacCallums in 1922, buying 5,800 tons and 7,600 tons respectively. MacCallums' sales in 1922,[22] totalling 48,500 tons (see Table 6.4 on page 76), were probably much less than 1921. Shipping income declined to £31,787 and the profit for the year was only £87 after transferring £54,000 to the ship replacement fund to match the catastrophic fall in the value of second hand tonnage.[23]

The recession deepened in 1923 with freight rates continuing their down-ward slide. Although steel prices bottomed out, demand for ship plates was

Ardgantock *unloading continental steel at Greenock in the early 1920s*

slack. MacCallums' merchant sales for the year halved to 23,747 tons.[24] Their business was only sustained by the continued custom of Workman Clark and Lithgows. Purchases declined correspondingly, dropping to 20,280 tons, with imports of 8,500 tons. About half the British steel was bought from Port Talbot, whose prices at £8.75 per ton compared unfavourably with European prices of £6.75 per ton.

The halving of merchant business resulted in a loss for the year of £3,274, after transferring a further £50,000 to the ship replacement fund. Shipping income dwindled to £17,661.[25] The outlook for coastal shipping did not justify maintaining seven vessels in commission. On 25 October 1923 the oldest ships, *Ardgarth* and *Ardgour*, built by George Brown & Co at Greenock just before the war, were sold for a total of £21,000.[26] Even at that low price the purchasers, the Northminster Steam Ship Co (Richards Longstaff & Co, London) took out mortgages from MacCallum which were redeemed in August 1924 and 30 June 1925. The vessels were named *Yorkminster* and *Yorkdale* by the new owners, but were quickly sold. During 1923 MacCallums had also to come to the aid of Workman Clark who were in serious financial difficulties with a moratorium being declared on their debenture stock. The directors of MacCallums agreed to purchase 2,500 of the company's shares from Workman Clark to help relieve the cash shortage and by so doing keep their most important customer in business.[27] This left only a small parcel of MacCallums' shares in the hands of the Workman Clark directors. At the same time MacCallums agreed to invest £7,000 in A & J Main & Co Ltd, a Glasgow firm of structural engineers and an established pre-war customers, 'provided they agreed to let us have all their enquiries for Iron and Steel and the preference or final refusal of any business in Iron and Steel and that we have the option of putting a director on the Board.'[28] Only one order, for 200 tons of steel, was placed as a result of this move.[29]

Table 6.2 Peter MacCallum & Sons Ltd – Profits, Provision for Taxation and Depreciation of Shipping 1920–45

Year	Net Profit	Provision for Taxation	Depreciation of Shipping
1919–20	− 6,957	—	—
1920–1	2,122	—	30,000
1921–2	87	—	54,000
1922–3	− 3,274	15,193	50,000
1923–4	13,008	—	50,000
1924–5	16,413	—	50,000
1925–6	985	—	47,500[1]
1926–7	29,676	—	25,144
1927–8	7,715	10,000	1,500
1928–9	8,304	—	1,500
1929–30	7,056	—	1,500
1930–1	1,313	—	—
1931–2	− 4,256	8,000	—
1932–3	− 9,713	7,728	—
1933–4	3,113	—	—
1934–5	2,504	—	—
1935–6	8,197	—	—[2]
1936–7	14,859	—	—
1937–8	3,470	—	—
1938–9	6,477	—	—
1939–40	15,566	—	—
1940–1	10,417	5,000	—
1941–2	10,155	6,500	—
1942–3	12,853	6,000	—
1943–4	13,906	—	—
1944–5	7,572	1,200	—

[1] *A further £30,000 was transferred from a separate reserve.*
[2] *£3,000 was applied from the sale of SS* Ardgarroch.
Note that in the 1920s dividends were paid free of tax: tax paid in this way has not been included. Between 1928 and 1931 £23,578 was written off the value of investments.
Source: *Directors' Reports in Minute Books.*

Although the dullness in the shipping market continued into 1924 many owners were beginning to consider new building on a modest scale to meet the upturn when it came. Shipbuilders, anxious to secure the business by quoting keen prices, inevitably looked to draw their steel from Europe. Because of Workman Clark's difficulties, MacCallums had to seek new customers. During the year over 64,000 tons of steel were sold, with only 3,800 tons going to Workman Clark.[30] Lithgows more than trebled their purchases from MacCallums taking 22,300 tons of continental steel at about £8.50 a ton, compared with a price of £9.75 a ton quoted to MacCallums by Lithgow's wholly-owned steelworks, Dunlops. MacCallums won a series of orders for German steel, totalling almost 6,000 tons, from Swan Hunter & Wigham Richardson, owners (jointly with Beardmore) of the Glasgow Iron & Steel Company. They also gained business from a number of independent engineers and shipbuilders including Clyde Shipbuilding and Engineering Co Ltd, of Port Glasgow, owned by Clan Line (6,610 tons); William Denny and Brothers of Dumbarton (3,000 tons) and Napier & Miller of Old

Table 6.3 Results from steamer operations: 1919–44

Date	Voyage Account £	Depreciation £	Ships' value
1919	41,048	12,000	296,500
1920	25,978	23,500	462,750[1]
1921	37,556	30,000	432,750
1922	31,787	54,500	300,144[2]
1923	17,661	50,000	250,144
1924	22,512	50,000	179,144
1925	15,180	50,000	129,144
1926	16,267	77,400[3]	51,644
1927	12,623	25,144	13,500[4]
1928	12,550	1,500	12,000
1929	12,571	1,500	10,500
1930	−314	1,500	9,000
1931	−2,276	0	9,000
1932	−3,936	0	9,000
1933	−1,390	0	9,000
1934	50	0	9,000
1935	688	0	6,000[5]
1936	1,034	0	3,000
1937	−396	0	3,000
1938	−1,377	0	3,000
1939	1,428	0	3,000
1940	9,019	0	3,000
1941	13,914	0	3,000
1942	10,441	0	3,000
1943	11,136	0	3,000
1944	11,001	0	3,000

Total: 294,755

[1] Ardglass *and* Ardgantock *delivered.*
[2] Ardgarroch *and* Ardgryfe *sold for £78,106.*
[3] *£30,000 additional depreciation transferred from reserve.*
[4] Ardgavel *sold for £13,000.*
[5] Ardglass *sold for £6,000.*

Kilpatrick (3,900 tons). The bulk of the merchant steel sold by MacCallums was drawn from the continent. Their imports totalled 59,380 tons, as opposed to only 13,680 tons from British makers. Nearly half the imported steel came through R H Ferguson of London. Of the British steel about a third came from Port Talbot, which was by then facing serious financial problems. The net profit for the year was £13,008, after transferring a further £50,000 to the ship replacement fund.

During the year MacCallums offered support to some of their customers who were badly hit by the recession. In April £2,000 was invested in a new company formed to carry on the business of H Buchanan & Co, ship chandlers and tinsmiths of Greenock.[31] (The connection with Buchanans lasted until the mid-1960s when John Burton Lang, son of J J Lang, took over the business moving out of ship chandling into the supply of hoteliers and caterers.[32]) Although never a large supplier to MacCallums, later in 1924 £4,000 was advanced to Motherwell Iron and Steel Co to prevent them from calling up the balance of their debenture stock. This action was taken on the initiative of the Glasgow firm of steel merchants P & W MacLellan.[33]

On 21 January 1924 James Fulton junior died at the early age of 44 in Torquay, where he had been wintering owing to poor health.[34] Although he had been responsible for the management of Lang & Fulton, he had also been a director of P MacCallum & Sons since its formation. A devotee of shooting and yachting, James Fulton junior was also interested in the Greenock Royal Infirmary, of which he was director, and was a trustee of Sir Gabriel Wood's Mariners Asylum, where, the *Greenock Telegraph* wrote, 'the old salts always found him a good friend'. He was replaced on the board by his brother, Charles Gibson Fulton, an insurance broker. It was the need for effective management of the insurance of the coastal fleet that made Charles Gibson's appointment desirable.

Since the war, James Fulton and Peter MacCallum Lang had continued to enlarge their underwriting business. In 1920 Charles Gibson Fulton, who was by then sole partner of the broking firm of McIntyre & Fulton, amalgamated his business with the old-established Glasgow underwriting firm of Rose Murison & Thomson, continuing that name. The syndicate formed by Charles Gibson Fulton in 1914 was integrated with a very large marine underwriting syndicate operated by Rose Murison and Thomson. The members brought in by C G Fulton included James and Henry Lithgow, James S Kincaid (managing director of the Ardrossan Shipbuilders Co and of John G. Kincaid & Co) as well as James Fulton and J J Lang, each initially taking a 3/62 share.[35] Men who should know state that membership of this syndicate was highly profitable. It had strong connections with the Far East where new trades, for instance in rubber, oil, and coir created new types of risk, with high premiums.

Flying Scud, *a Fulton family yacht, on passage to Oban in the mid-1920s. Both the Fulton and Lang families were keen yachtsmen.*

During 1925, MacCallums' purchases of steel fell by 40 per cent to 51,000 tons.[36] This movement reflected a general downturn in the economy and a reduction of prices. Surprisingly, however, profits rose. The net return for the year was £16,413 after allowing a further £50,000 for ship replacement.[37] During the year MacCallums again came to the succour of Workman Clark which was now in deep trouble as the Northumberland Shipbuilding Group was on the verge of breakdown.[38] The directors agreed to buy from Workman Clark £13,500 £1 shares held in Baldwins Ltd, selling half of them on to Sir Charles Wright, now a director of Baldwins.[39] At the same time MacCallums, in conjunction with the Glasgow marine engineering firm of David Rowan & Co (a significant customer), invested £3,500 in John Marshall & Co (Motherwell) Ltd, boilermakers.[40]

At the beginning of 1926 the worst of the depression seemed to be past. Freight rates crept up, and shipowners began to place orders for new tonnage. Serious industrial unrest, culminating in the General Strike in May and the ensuing prolonged coal strike, severely disrupted the domestic steel industry. Scottish ingot output fell from 1,074,600 tons in 1925 to only 473,000 tons.[41] This gave MacCallums an excellent opportunity to market continental steel. Before the strike the company was placing large contracts with both British and continental producers[42] for example 15,000 tons were ordered from Consett Iron Company's new works between January and March, 3,000 tons each from Gutehoffnungshütte and Montangesellschaft; and 4,000 tons from the Societe Anonyme des Forges et Ateliers de Dilling. After May nearly all the steel came from the continent. Between July and December 1926 no less than 31,000 tons of steel was ordered from R H Ferguson, the London firm of steel importers. The total imports for the year were 58,125 tons, as compared with only 26,588 tons of home produced steel. Sales reached a peak of 102,257 tons, double the previous year's total, with Lithgows taking a third.

Table 6.4 *Analysis of steel sales by customers: 1922–33*

	Lithgows	Workman Clark	Cammell Laird	Scotts Shipbuilding & Engineering	Total
1922	7,600	16,200	5,500	9,350	49,535
1923	7,300	11,462	0	300	23,747
1924	22,300	3,800	5,700	4,800	64,351
1925	22,550	9,475	0	50	51,065
1926	33,700	13,000	11,500	450	102,257[1]
1927	1,000	0	18,900	4,900	75,919
1928	12,490	32,090	12,520	0	70,187
1929	3,500	35,500	49,400	5,150	133,367
1930	0	0	0	345	16,236
1931	0	2,562	0	0	5,625
1932	0	0	0	390	2,485
1933	0	17,400	0	2,200	23,450

[1] *117,500 tons of steel was returned during the year.*

This success was reflected in a profit in 1925 of £985 after £47,500 had been allowed for ship replacement.[43]

By the autumn of 1926 there were signs that the boom was only transient and that some builders had ordered continental steel as a precaution. Mac-Callums agreed with D & W Henderson, Cammell Laird, the Clyde Ship-building & Engineering Co and the Ardrossan Dockyard Co to purchase from them 117,500 tons of continental steel ordered during that year.[44] Of equal concern to MacCallums must have been the collapse of the Northumberland Shipbuilding Group[45] and the closure of the Port Talbot Steel-works.[46] The Northumberland Group was reconstructed as the Shipbuilders Investment Co, which was designed by Clarence Hatry as a vehicle for rationalizing the shipbuilding industry.[47] The new concern acquired the assets of Workman Clark (including Lanarkshire Steel), the Fairfield Ship-building & Engineering Co, the Monmouth Shipbuilding Co, William Dox-ford & Son, the Irvine Shipbuilding & Dry Dock Co and the Blythswood Shipbuilding Co. The new group continued to place business with MacCal-lums. During the year, the Blythswood yard ordered 3,850 tons of British steel from the company. By the end of December 1926 Workman Clark were seeking to settle their accounts by bills, to which MacCallums reluctantly agreed, though in the event the facility was not used.[48] At a much more modest level, a guarantee of £50 was given, by MacCallums, in April 1926 to the Clydesdale Bank's Gourock branch on account of Hugh Ramsay & Co blockmakers, Gourock, an established customer of MacCallums' stock-holding department.[49]

Despite the large re-purchase of steel at the end of 1926, results for 1927 were better than might have been expected. Sales totalled 75,919 tons, of which 46,250 tons were new purchases from the continent.[50] A post-war record net profit of £29,676 was declared, even after allowing £25,144 to be transferred to the ship replacement reserve.[51] Shipping income returned to a downward trend, falling by nearly a quarter during the year to £12,623. The *Ardgarvel*, built in 1917 by Ferguson Brothers, Port Glasgow, was, therefore, sold for £13,500 to J H Welford & Co Ltd, who quickly passed her to Union Steamship Ltd, Vancouver.[52] This left a fleet of four vessels built in 1918–9, the *Ardgantock*, *Ardgarroch*, *Ardglass* and *Ardgryfe;* there being no incentive to buy new vessels either to reduce costs or to expand the volume of trade.

At the end of 1927 the future of the trade in foreign steel, the mainstay of MacCallums' merchant business, was uncertain. The budget of 1927 allowed the 'Big Four' railway companies to vary their rates of carriage thus permit-ting British steelmakers to quote lower delivered prices. Scottish, North East and Midland steelmakers combined to introduce a rebate scheme for ship-building steel which would, it was hoped, result in the exclusion of foreign steel. Merchants who supplied steel through the scheme were to receive commissions. So as to qualify as participants MacCallums were obliged to join the Glasgow Iron Merchants Association, whose prices they had consistently undercut since its formation in 1900.[53] At the same time the Glasgow Iron Merchants Association combined with other regional groups to form the Steel Merchants Association to provide a united front in negotiations with the steel makers.[54] These developments almost certainly led the directors of MacCallums to re-appraise the capitalization of the company.

There was little likelihood of new shipping tonnage being required by the company, and the steel merchanting and stockholding business was not making heavy demands on capital. It was, therefore, suggested that the company should be wound up and a new company formed, as was done by Workman Clark in the following year. However, on detailed examination it was found preferable to reduce the capital from the £250,000 of the heady days of 1918 to a more realistic value of £75,000. This was achieved by returning to the shareholders £7 for each of the 25,000 £10 shares, reducing the nominal value of the shares to £3, and then by dividing each £3 share into three £1 shares. This intention was confirmed at a series of meetings in January and February 1928, and authorized by the Court of Session in May.[55] To pay out the shareholders, Government stock to the nominal value of £146,000 from the ship replacement fund was realized at just over par. The shareholders in June 1928 were:

Peter MacCallum Lang	17,616
Louis Vandalle Fulton	19,890
John James Lang	14,934
John Fulton	6,630
Charles Gibson Fulton	6,630
John Dunlop Dempster	600
Charles McKinlay Duncan	600
William Strachan	600
Kingston Investment Co	3,750
Sir William Charles Wright	3 750

Thus the Lang family holding of 32,550 shares was just exceeded by the Fulton one of 33,150. Later in the month Sir William Charles Wright's shares were purchased by the MacCallum directors.[56] The capital remained at £75,000 for only a few months, as in October 1928 it was agreed to capitalize £10,000 in the reserve account, and distribute it to the shareholders *pro rata*.[57] This was followed in November by a complicated series of transactions in which the major shareholders transferred part of their holdings to the minority shareholders and others. In particular J D Dempster acquired 3,867 shares from Peter M Lang and John J Lang, reflecting his growing importance in the company. In January 1929 Peter M. Lang transferred a further 4,000 shares to his son Ian MacCallum Lang signifying his active involvement in the management of MacCallums. The aim of these trans-

78

fers, which has continued to the present, was to maintain a rough balance between the Lang and Fulton family holdings.

The rebate scheme and lower railway rates had the effect desired by the British steelmakers. During 1928 MacCallums purchased 62,810 tons of steel of which only 16,260 tons were of continental make, the lowest total since 1923.[58] Sales remained stable at 70,187 tons with almost 12,500 tons being taken by Lithgows and 32,090 tons by the reconstructed Workman Clark (1928) Ltd. Profits, however, were depressed reflecting generally lower margins. Net profits were £7,715 with only £1,500 being allowed for ship replacement. After the reconstruction of the balance sheet the company still held investments valued at £27,547, transferred from the ship replacement fund. Most of these were 'investments by way of trade'.[59] During the year the Shipbuilders Investment Co had failed and Workman Clark (1928) Ltd had been formed by the Strachan brothers. MacCallums invested £25,000 in the new concern.[60]

The increasing volume of world seaborne trade and the belief, based on pre-war experience, that the worst of the depression must be over, led to a substantial rise in the number of shipbuilding contracts during 1929. The desire of shipbuilders to secure adequate supplies of steel led to forward contracts being placed. This resulted in MacCallums ordering 172,000 tons of steel, over 10 per cent of total Scottish ingot make,[61] and more than twice the previous post-war peak in 1926. All but 18,500 tons of this was of British make. Sales totalled 133,367 tons. With Workman Clark taking 25,000 tons and Cammell Laird 49,400. Lithgows only purchased 3,500 tons. Despite this enormous volume of business, net profits were only £8,304, with £1,500 going to ship replacement.[62]

During 1929 MacCallums lost its first chairman, James Fulton, and in the following year (on 26 April) its current chairman, Peter MacCallum Lang. James Fulton had been retired for twenty years, and had been in poor health for two years before his death. Apart from his involvement as partner in Lang and Fulton; and partner, later chairman, of MacCallums, he had been interested in the Greenock Provident Bank and the Greenock Chamber of Commerce. According to his obituary in the *Greenock Telegraph*,[63] 'Quiet and unobtrusive, he was a generous giver in many ways and was held in high esteem in the community.' Peter MacCallum Lang, was, like James Fulton, a modest person, but a man of considerable business ability. He was a director of the Greenock firm of John G Kincaid & Co Ltd and of John Hastie & Co Ltd as well as being a director of Lang & Fulton: and partner, later director, in MacCallums. His influence on the fortunes of both the shipping and the steel side of the business from the 1890s was critical. During the First World War he was involved in the control of steel in the Clyde District, and was offered a knighthood for his services, which he declined as he did not wish to be honoured on account of the war.[64] He was a man of wide interests, being a staunch member of St Paul's Church, an active cricketer in his earlier years

Peter MacCallum Lang, who died in 1930

and a former president of Greenock Cricket Club, and a director of Greenock Provident Bank (now incorporated in the West of Scotland Trustee Savings Bank). Like James Fulton, he was a benevolent man. According to a note in St Paul's Church Magazine, 'he was one of the most generous and big hearted of men in our town, and his generosity had this added virtue that it was so often given unsolicited'. His sudden death was, therefore, a blow not only to MacCallums, but also to the town of Greenock as a whole. His loss was felt outside the town, as his obituary in the *Glasgow Herald*[65] indicated.

The new chairman of MacCallums was Louis Vandalle Fulton, James Fulton's eldest son. He was immediately faced with the worst conditions the company had ever experienced.

Hurricane

During 1930 orders placed for steel by MacCallums collapsed to just over 5,000 tons, and sales dwindled to 16,236 tons – about 12 per cent of the previous year's total.[66] A loss was made on the voyage account, though a net profit of £7,056 was made on shipping operations. The shipping department was not immediately affected, as orders placed in 1929 continued to be delivered during 1930 when, indeed, the tonnage launched from Clyde and Belfast yards was maintained at a high level. At this time of crisis, MacCal-

P M Lang's home 'Lindores' above Greenock, built for a
member of the Lyle family

lums must have been troubled by Sir James Lithgow's growing involvement in high level steel politics, symptomatic of a general regrouping and rationalization among both suppliers and customers.[67]

In this manœuvring Sir James and Henry Lithgow used their bargaining power as major customers for steel to secure ends which they believed desirable not only from their own point of view but also from a national Scottish standpoint. The Lithgow vision of a fully integrated Scottish steel industry to be created economically from existing assets was a compelling one, one that drove Sir James into strange byways while Henry held the fort in the shipyards. The negotiations were well under way in 1929 (reflected in low purchases from MacCallums) and were brought to a head in 1930 with an agreement to amalgamate James Dunlop & Co's outdated and heavily-indebted Calderbank Steel Works with the dynamic empire of David Colville & Sons Ltd, to form Colvilles Ltd with effect from 1 January 1931. Calderbank, having served its turn as a bargaining counter, was immediately put out of production. Agreements by Lithgows and Harland & Wolff[68] to purchase all their steel from Colvilles ensured relative prosperity for the new concern despite the appallingly low level of demand, though the collapse of the Royal Mail Group and prosecution of Lord Kylsant did not help.[69] This relatively good performance put the new combine in a good position to exert pressure on the remaining Scottish steelmakers, but in the event it was Sir James Lithgow personally, with Bank of England support, who negotiated their integration. The first to come into the fold was William Beardmore & Co.[70] As part of the price for survival of the nucleus of the Beardmore empire at Parkhead, Lithgow arranged for the transfer of that company's shipbuilding steel business to Colvilles Ltd in April 1934. He then went on in July 1934 to acquire personally, with Bank of England finance, a controlling interest in the Steel Company of Scotland. Lithgow obtained control with its possibility of an alternative source of supply for the family shipyards, partly as a gambit to force a reluctant Colville board to cooperate with the Steel Company of Scotland. Once a successful share issue in Colvilles had been made in March 1936, that company was able, among other purchases, to acquire the Steel Company of Scotland from Lithgows. Negotiations were then completed in July 1936 for the acquisition of the Lanarkshire Steel Company, concentrating all the major Scottish steel works in the hands of Colvilles. No longer would merchants like MacCallums bargain with individual Scottish producers; henceforth they faced a unitary supplier of heavy products, though the old company names were retained. The last orders were placed with James Dunlop & Co in 1929, with Lanarkshire in 1936, and the last substantial orders with the Steel Company of Scotland in the same year.[71]

MacCallums' English and Welsh suppliers were also affected by the rationalization moves made in response to the critical financial position of many producers by the end of the 1920s. Port Talbot was affected by the amalgamation of Baldwins with Guest Keen in 1930 to form Guest Keen Baldwins Iron & Steel Co,[72] and Dorman Long in 1929 absorbed Bolckow Vaughan,[73] though a proposed takeover of Cargo Fleet did not materialize. The long connection with Port Talbot ended in 1936 partly as a result of the collapse of Workman Clark and the sale by Lithgows of their shares in 1934, and, partly as a consequence of a regional pricing scheme introduced in 1936.[74] MacCallums' business with Colvilles tailed off after 1936. Instead MacCallums looked to the North East steelmakers, Dorman Long, to meet their needs. They had first sold steel (5,100 tons) to MacCallums in 1929, and became after 1934 their steadiest suppliers.[75]

While the reorganization of the British steel industry was in progress, British shipbuilding was suffering from an unparalleled depression which hit companies already in trouble owing to the lower-than-expected demand for ships in the 1920s. The underlying problem of overcapacity in the industry had resulted in low levels of profitability throughout the 1920s, and the exhaustion of reserves accumulated during previous periods of prosperity. The ending in 1928 of Government-guaranteed loans to shipowners under the Trades Facilities Acts[77] exacerbated the effects of the depression in freight rates which resulted from the collapse of international trade in 1929. Even before the depression had begun to bite, Sir James Lithgow, Sir Andrew Duncan (former vice-president of the Shipbuilders Employers' Federation), J E Thirlaway (chairman of Swan Hunter) and John Barr, met Montagu Norman, Governor of the Bank of England on 24 April 1929 to discuss 'an association charged with the task of securing the closure of uneconomic yards which might be purchased by a holding company'.[78] The idea was that the cost of acquisition would be financed by a levy of 1 per cent on the contract or the sale price of vessels launched. This plan reached fruition in March 1930 with the registration of National Shipbuilders Security Ltd.[79] The first sale to the new company was Beardmore's Dalmuir Yard, never more than a casual customer of MacCallums. The former Caird Yard of Harland & Wolff, not a MacCallums contact since its takeover in 1916, followed. More seriously for MacCallums, Napier and Miller of Old Kilpatrick, regular purchasers of steel from MacCallums, sold out to NSS, and as the depression deepened, D & W Henderson of Meadowside gave up shipbuilding.[80] After prolonged negotiations their ship repair business was acquired by Harland & Wolff in 1936. Most seriously for MacCallums, the reconstructed Workman Clark (1928) Ltd was forced into liquidation, and its yard was sold to NSS in 1935. These closures and the formal agreements made by Lithgows and Harland & Wolff to take their steel supplies directly from Colvilles Ltd represented a serious loss of both actual and potential custom to MacCallums.[81]

The effect of the recession on MacCallums' business was catastrophic. From 1931 to 1933 no new steel was purchased, and only 31,560 tons were sold, almost all of it contracted for in 1929.[82] Nearly half of these sales were accounted for by the last orders from Workman Clark in 1933. Shipping slumped severely. The value of the fleet had been written down from £86,144

Louis Vandalle Fulton

in 1927 to £9,000 by 1930. Between 1931 and 1933 losses were made on the voyage account in every year.[83]

During 1932 the steamers were laid up for most of the year, and at the annual Ordinary General Meeting of the company in December, the chairman, L V Fulton, reported that 'the Shipping Department had a very hard time'.[84] By 1933 the overall profit and loss account had a negative balance of £9,713. No allowance for depreciation could in the circumstances be made. With business at a very low level the directors had no alternative to reducing costs. Mrs McLaren, who started as a typist in the shipping office in 1926, recalled fifty years later that in 1931 the company had to pay off three typists, a clerk and a clerkess. A notice from the Board dated 3 April 1931 referred to part time working, two weeks on and one week off, with only statutory local holidays allowed. This arrangement, coupled with weekly payment of salaries, allowed the affected staff to draw unemployment benefit for the weeks off. In the midst of these difficulties Ian MacCallum Lang, Peter MacCallum Lang's eldest son, was appointed a director, at the age of twenty-four, and in 1934 6,902 of his late father's shares were transferred to him.

Calmer Seas

By the end of 1933 the outlook was beginning to improve, though only 200 tons of steel were purchased in that year. At the Ordinary General Meeting in December 1933 L V Fulton commented from the chair that the steamers 'are all commissioned at present and the outlook for them for the coming year is decidedly better'.[85] On the steel side MacCallums could no longer expect to take advantage of lower continental prices. In 1932 the National Government, responding to pressure from the steel industry, imposed duties ranging from 20 to $33\frac{1}{3}$ per cent on imported steel.[86] MacCallums therefore had to adopt a more aggressive approach to marketing steel and other metals if they were to survive in business. A further complicating factor was the introduction of a regional selling scheme by the steelmakers in 1936. Steel merchants and sheet merchants, concerned that this plan would deprive them of business, formed the Steel Distributors Association, with the support of Sir Andrew Duncan, by then chairman of the newly formed British Iron & Steel Federation. MacCallums joined this new association[87]; but were unable, because of the scheme, to continue supplying Cammell Laird. Ian M Lang at once became an active member of the Association.

It proved impossible for MacCallums to find new markets for steel capable of absorbing the tonnages which had been sold in the better years of the 1920s. However, some new outlets emerged, including the Ailsa Shipbuilding Co, Troon, and Lobnitz & Co, Renfrew, taking 2,655 tons and 1,659 tons respectively in 1935/6.[88] What must have been determined attempts to break into new markets led to the supply of pig iron to the Caledonian Foundry Co, Greenock, which had strong links with Hasties. There was also a temporarily successful movement into the supply of steel reinforcement bars to contractors for reinforced concrete structures. This lasted from 1936 to 1938, when the desire for formed reinforcement made the trade unattractive to general merchants like MacCallums. The supply of non-ferrous ingots to Barr & Co (Brass Founders) Ltd, Greenock, also a Hastie subsidiary, began in 1937 and this company became one of MacCallums steadiest clients. For a short period between 1935 and 1939 the company supplied tinplate to John Drummond & Son, their next-door neighbours in Rue End Street. Baldwins Ltd, Swansea, contracted for about 60,000 boxes of tin plate between 1935 and 1939. Throughout the late 1930s, however, established customers provided a low-level, but important, basic demand. William Denny & Bros (taking 24,484 tons from 1934 to 1939), John G. Kincaid & Co (7,990 tons), George Brown & Co (9,764 tons), and Barclay Curle & Co (50,490 tons), remained the major consumers of MacCallums steel. Ferguson Brothers of Port Glasgow took 2,890 tons. This connection was reinforced by the marriage of Ian MacCallum Lang to Margaret Helen Ferguson, daughter of Robert Ferguson, one of the founding partners.

Within this framework of demand, MacCallums were for a time remarkably successful. Purchases of steel rose to 21,676 tons in 1934, 47,768 tons in 1935 and 48,983 tons in 1936. Sales in 1934 amounted to 28,428 tons, in 1935 to 35,645 tons and in 1936 to 53,416 tons. In 1937, however, both purchases and sales slumped badly, to just over 8,000 tons, and the market did not recover substantially before the outbreak of war.

The shipping side of the business did not recover as quickly as the merchanting of steel. The voyage account only recorded a surplus of £1,772 between 1934 and 1936. In 1935 the *Ardglass* was sold for £6,000 to Messrs Monroe Bros Ltd, Liverpool.[89] This vessel, which had been built in 1919 by J Fullerton & Co, Paisley, was renamed *Kyle Castle*. By 1936 the shipping market had improved sufficiently to encourage MacCallums to invest £6,000 in the Kindiesel Shipping Co,[90] formed to acquire and run experimentally a small coaster built by the Ardrossan Dockyard Co and powered by a new type of diesel engine modified from a Harland & Wolff design by Kincaids (see below). MacCallums were appointed managers to the new company; a similar relationship to that between Lang & Fulton and its single-ship companies a generation earlier. In August 1936, perhaps to concentrate custom on the new vessel, MacCallums sold the *Ardgarroch*, built by the Ardrossan Dry Dock and Shipbuilding Co in 1918.[91] She was purchased by the Mersey Ports and Stevedoring Co Ltd, Liverpool through Messrs S C Chambers & Co, shipbrokers, for £6,000.

The departure of the *Ardgarroch* left MacCallums with only two vessels of their own, the *Ardgantock* and the *Ardgryfe*. These had mixed fortunes during 1937 and 1938 with the voyage account accumulating a loss of £1,773. At the end of 1937 it was reported that they had 'experienced a certain amount of misfortune involving heavy repairs coupled with time charters which prevented them taking advantage of the increased rates.'[92] The *Ard-*

gryfe, for example, was between March 1936 and May 1938 on time charter on the London to Antwerp run, with general cargo.[93] A sharp recession in trade in 1938 led to a difficult year for the steamers, with a lack of cargo and a fall in rates leading to their laying up.[94]

The improvement in business restored the company to profitability. In 1934 a net profit of £3,113 was recorded which was applied to reduce the debt.[95] In 1934–5 the deficit was further reduced by £2,504. In 1936 it was cancelled and after allowing £3,000 to reserve there was a credit of £1,529. The position improved still more in 1936–7, when after allowing £6,000 to reserve there was a profit of £8,859, which allowed a payment of a $7\frac{1}{2}$% dividend, the first since 1931. The downturn in trade of 1938 predictably hit profits, which were down to £3,470, but a $3\frac{1}{2}$% dividend was paid. The

Table 6.5 *Extract from Abstract Log of SS* Ardgantock

Sailed from	Date	Arrived at	Date	Cargo
Blyth	10.3.36	Whitby	12.3.36	Coal
Whitby	9.4.36	Sunderland	9.4.36	Ballast
Sunderland	27.5.36	Seaham	27.5.36	Ballast
Seaham	29.5.36	Cowes	1.6.36	Coal
Cowes	6.6.36	Havre	6.6.36	Ballast
Havre	10.6.36	Avonmouth	13.6.36	Grain
Avonmouth	16.6.36	Runcorn	17.6.36	Ballast
Runcorn	19.6.36	Wick	22.6.36	Salt
Peterhead	26.6.36	Granton	27.6.36	Ballast
Granton	29.6.36	Nakskov	3.7.36	Coal and coke
Nakskov	7.7.36	Gdynia	8.7.36	Ballast
Gdynia	11.7.36	Sunderland	16.7.36	D.B.B.
Sunderland	21.7.36	Middlesbrough	21.7.36	Ballast
Middlesbrough	21.7.36	Amsterdam	23.7.36	Coal
Amsterdam	23.7.36	Brussels	25.7.36	Ballast
Brussels	29.7.36	Goole	31.7.36	Scrap
Goole	4.8.36	Leith	6.8.36	Ballast

Source: *Abstract Log Book.*

company, with its two steamers written down to £3,000 and reserves of £12,000, was thus in a sound position to face the growing threat of war.

As soon as the company began to turn round, its pilot through the difficult years, Louis Vandalle Fulton, died suddenly at the age of 55.[96] He had been closely identified with the Glasgow-Renfrewshire Association, a benevolent society. His favourite hobby was yachting, and he had been a member of the Royal Northern, Royal Clyde and Clyde Corinthian Yacht Clubs and the Clyde Cruising Club. The elder of his two sons, James Vandalle Fulton, succeeded him on the board, in August 1934, and John James Lang replaced him as chairman. 9,641 of L V Fulton's shares were transferred to James V Fulton in April 1935, and at the same time 6,902 of P M Lang's shares went to his second son, James Fulton Lang, who had followed his uncle C G Fulton into the marine insurance firm of Rose Murison & Thomson in 1932, becoming a partner in 1936.[97] Charles Gibson Fulton did not

John James (J J) Lang

long survive his brother L V, dying in December 1936. His shares were divided between his nephews, James V Fulton (3,511) and Robert Waterston Fulton (3,510). R W Fulton also received his part of his father's shareholding (9,641 shares) in May 1937.[63]

The younger generation were quickly precipitated into positions of power. John James Lang died suddenly in 1937 at the age of sixty.[98] As well as being Chairman of MacCallums, he was also Chairman of John Hastie & Co Ltd. Like his brother, Peter, he had been a director of the Greenock Provident Bank, and like James Fulton, a director of Greenock Royal Infirmary. At the time of his death he was captain of the Kilmacolm Golf Club. In December 1936 he had transferred 5,000 of his shares to his son, John Burton Lang, and the remaining 5,521 shares were passed to J B Lang in October 1937. Ian MacCallum Lang replaced him as Chairman. At the end of that year Charles MacKinlay Duncan, who had been a director since 1920, decided to retire. He was granted a pension, later changed to a consultancy fee,[99] and sold his shareholding in March 1938 to Ian M Lang (7,500) J V Fulton (1,250) and R W Fulton (1,250). In the following month the places on the board vacated by J J Lang and C M Duncan were taken by R W Fulton and John Burton Lang, who until then had been very much engaged in his own packaging business, and who returned to it early in 1939.[100] Further

Ardmillan House, near Girvan in Ayrshire, left to Mrs P M Lang by her brother James Fulton junior. A shooting party outside the house in the early 1930s with second from left Charles Gibson Fulton, a guest, Ian MacCallum Lang, and James Fulton Lang.

concentration of shares in the hands of the Lang and Fulton families took place later in the year when the shareholdings of Laurence Crawford (460) and William Strachan (680) were divided among Ian M Lang, J V Fulton and R W Fulton in the proportions 2:1:1. The effect of all these changes was to put the management of the company in young hands, with the able and experienced support of John D Dempster.

The Second World War did not offer the same opportunities to shipowners or industrialists as had the first. The Government, from experience gained in managing large-scale hostilities between 1914 and 1919, had retained an effective team of advisers on the control of procurement and transport through the Principal Supply Officers' Committee and its subcommittees. Control of metal supplies and shipping passed immediately to the Government.[101]

At the outbreak of war, MacCallums' biggest problem was the immediate mobilization of nearly all the senior management. Ian M Lang, John B Lang, J V Fulton and R W Fulton joined their units, along with James F Lang, the insurance broker.[102] The serious gap this created in the direction of the company was partially filled by the appointment of Hugh Crawford Waterston, uncle of the young Fultons, as a director.[103] H C Waterston was Vice Chairman of the Scottish Iron & Steel Company Ltd, a supplier to MacCallums, and when that concern was merged with the iron and steel interests of William Baird & Co in 1939, he became Vice Chairman of the new company, Bairds & Scottish Steel Ltd. He became qualified as a director of MacCallums by the transfer of 1,000 shares from R W Fulton, and represented the interests of the Fultons throughout the war, acting as chairman of the company. The main burden of day to day decision-making, however, fell on John D Dempster, though after John B Lang was demobilized in 1940 he gave part-time assistance until May 1941 when he again resigned. It is certainly easy to believe that Mr Dempster's vote of thanks at the 1939 General Meeting was heartfelt. He 'expressed the hope that it would not be long till the present crisis is over and all who have been called up in the national service were safely back again'. A sign of the pressure on the staff during the war was the regular adjournment of the General Meetings from the pre-war December dates to February or even March.[104]

An immediate consequence of the outbreak of war was a swift rise in freight and insurance rates. The *Kindiesel*, for example, which was carrying coal during the early months of 1939 at 4s. 6d. to 7s. 6d. per ton was by November earning 13s. per ton and by April 1940 21s. 6d. per ton.[105] However, by December 1940 John Dempster reported that the *Ardgantock* had been requisitioned by the Admiralty though the *Ardgryfe* was still 'trading free'. Two steamers, the *Nordost* and *Ophir* had been allocated to MacCallums by the Ministry of Shipping for management. A third vessel, the aged *Margo* was also transferred to the company on 30 November 1940.[106] The voyage account for 1939–40 showed a healthy balance of £15,566.[107] Throughout 1941 *Ardgantock* remained in Admiralty control, being used as an armed store carrier, while the *Ardgryfe* was requisitioned by the Ministry of War Transport on 23 June 1941.[108] The vessel remained with MacCallums, but the Ministry gave specific instructions for chartering. Between 1942 and 1945 she was principally engaged in coal carrying.[109] On 30 May 1941 a new motor coaster, the *Empire Bank* of 402 gross tons was allocated to the company. This vessel had been built by Henry Scarr Ltd of Hessle.[110] Her arrival brought the number of 'foreign' ships managed to four. The profit on the voyage account for 1940–1 amounted to £13,914.[111]

At the end of 1942 the management of the *Empire Bank* was transferred to Metcalfe Motor Coasters Ltd, London, who in 1946 absorbed her into their own fleet as the *Rose Julie M*.[112] As a result, profits from the shipping business dropped back to £10,441, remaining at this level until 1944,[113] when the three vessels still being managed for the Ministry of War Transport were transferred to the Kindiesel Shipping Co (see below), and the directors began to consider 'the advisability of replacing the company's shipping tonnage to meet post-war requirements'.[114]

On the iron and steel side of the business the Ministry of Supply took control of orders, restricting merchants' activities. Good contact with existing customers was maintained until 1941–2, when tighter controls of merchant business were introduced.[115] The stock trade, however, continued to receive adequate supplies, and 'continued its function in doing excellent service in the district to the various firms engaged greatly in national work of importance.'[116] Though no figures survive the stock department seems to have been busy throughout the war. During 1944 merchanting revived as the end of the war came in sight. To meet the increasing demand for stock, 4,600 square yards of ground at Mackenzie Street, Greenock (the present stockyard) was bought for £2,863.[117]

Overall profits were much better than the average for the thirties. Between 1939 and 1945 they did not drop below £10,000 per annum. Dividends were maintained at 10%, the maximum permitted by the Government. Liability for taxation was reduced by allowances for wear and tear, and by an upward revision of the Excess Profits tax allowance.[118]

The even performance of the business contrasted tragically with the fate of the senior managers serving in the armed forces.[119] On 12 April 1943 MacCallums suffered a grievous loss when Major R W (Robin) Fulton was killed in action in Tunisia. He had been with the 77th Field Regiment of the Royal Artillery observing the fire of the guns, when he was killed by a mortar bomb. At about the same time Ian MacCallum Lang was seriously injured in the shoulder while in action, and was demobilized. He had served with the rank of Major in the same regiment as his cousin Robin Fulton, and with William Wallace, a MacCallum clerk, as his battery sergeant. He had survived the evacuation from Dunkirk, where he was one of the last off the beaches. On that occasion he had to abandon a smart new pair of boots to swim out to the rescue boat, but saved his briefcase, containing regimental papers, by tying it round his neck. He continued to use that briefcase for the rest of his working life. It is also worth recording that when they went to the war Ian Lang and Robin Fulton were each drawing an annual salary of £250 from MacCallums. From the time of Robin's death until his own, nearly forty years later, Ian refused any increase in salary for his work in the company owned by the two families.

Ian Lang's brother, James Fulton Lang, joined the RAF and commanded an Air Sea Rescue launch for most of the war. He was based for a time at Dover and his was the only launch to return out of five that took part in the Dieppe raid in 1942. Later, in the Mediterranean, his boat rescued a total of 54 Allied aircrew in two years. He was awarded the DSC for one such rescue, under heavy enemy fire, off Sardinia. He spent the last six months of the war in charge of the shore station at St Tropez, a village in the south of France, where a local publican, Mme Madu, re-opened her sea-front bar, renaming it Jimmy's Bar in his honour!

The war ended sadly for MacCallums. R V Fulton's brother, Lieutenant Commander James V Fulton, RNVR, was killed off Murmansk on 29 April 1945, a week before the end of hostilities, when the frigate he was commanding, *HMS Goodall*, was torpedoed, hit in the magazine and blew up. He was thirty five, only six years married, with three young children. The company then had lost two of the three young men who had planned in the late 1930s to take it into the future, and the third, Ian M Lang, had suffered wounds which were to continue to trouble him for many years. A whole generation of Fultons had been wiped out.

James V Fulton, who was killed in action in 1945

The Kindiesel Experiment

The Kindiesel Shipping Co[120] had its origin in a verbal agreement between the directors of the MacCallums with John G Kincaid & Co to form a company to acquire for £12,500 the *Kindiesel*, a vessel built to test a new type of small marine diesel engine designed by Kincaid. The company had 135 shares of £100 each allocated to the two companies (66 to MacCallums and 65 to Kincaids) and one each to James Scott Kincaid and Robert Greer as directors of Kincaids and John James Lang and James Vandalle Fulton as directors of MacCallums. Initially the Clydesdale Bank, Glasgow, held the MacCallum shares as nominees. The company's first meeting was in August 1936, and the vessel went into service in September of that year. The first months of operation were affected by machinery trouble, and over a thirteen month period the vessel was out of service for $45\frac{1}{2}$ days, 'a very serious item in a one ship company'. The loss on this period was £285. The vessel traded mainly in china clay and coal. The managers reported in October 1937 that 'the engine has, we feel sure, as an economical running unit amply justified Mr. Kincaid's hopes – the fuel consumption having averaged 16.5 cwt per day'. Another factor affecting the profitability of the vessel was the lower rates of freight for smaller coasters than for the larger steam vessels. The next year's results were similar, though the loss through machinery trouble was reduced to 30 days. Freight rates dropped by about a third from April. The managers accepted freights which in some cases did not show any balance for profit or depreciation, as it was their intention 'to run this vessel as much as possible in view of the new type of machinery with which she is fitted'. They

Table 6.6 Extract from Abstract Log of MV Kindiesel

Sailed from	Date	Arrived at	Date	Cargo
Ardrossan	26.8.36	Ayr	26.8.36	Ballast[1]
Ayr (via Wemyss Bay)	28.8.36	Charlestown	30.8.36	Coal
Charlestown	5.9.36	Larne	7.9.36	Bagged china clay
Larne	8.9.36	Ayr	8.9.36	Ballast
Ayr	9.9.36	Ardrossan	9.9.36	Ballast
Ardrossan	10.9.36	Charlestown	12.9.36	Coal
Charlestown	15.9.36	Teinmouth	16.9.36	Ballast
Teignmouth	17.9.36	Antwerp	19.9.36	China clay
Antwerp	24.9.36	Stranraer	29.9.36	Fertilizers
Stranraer	1.10.36	Girvan	1.10.36	Fertilizers
Girvan	2.10.36	Ayr	2.10.36	Ballast
Ayr	2.10.36	Ardrossan	2.10.36	Ballast
Ardrossan	3.10.36	Ayr	3.10.36	Ballast
Ayr	6.10.36	Charlestown	7.10.36	Coal
Charlestown	14.10.36	Larne	16.10.36	Bagged china clay
Larne	19.10.36	Dublin	20.10.36	Ballast
Dublin	20.10.36	Belfast	21.10.36	Scrap
Belfast	21.10.36	Newcastle	25.10.36	Scrap
Newcastle	3.11.36	Blyth	3.11.36	Ballast
Blyth	3.11.36	Ramsgate	6.11.36	Coal

Source: *Abstract Log.*
[1] *Maiden voyage.*

reported 'extreme slackness in all trades', and MacCallums as managers had reduced their fee by 50 per cent to help the Kindiesel Company 'through these difficult times'.

At the end of the first two years, the vessel was completely overhauled at Ardrossan, and was out of action for about six months. She resumed service in March 1939 and from then until 30 September carried 27 cargoes at a loss of £150 without losing any time for machinery faults. After the outbreak of war, freight rates did not rise immediately to cover the additional costs of wartime operation, but by the end of September a reasonable increase had taken place. Clearly the problems of running a single-ship company had

MV Kindiesel

become serious, for in July an agreement was reached with the Ardrossan Dockyard Ltd for the construction of a steel single-screw cargo vessel of 1,500 tons. Experience with the diesel engine had obviously been unhappy, for the proposed vessel was to be steam propelled. The first full year of wartime operation was disappointing. Insurance premiums were very heavy, and accounted for about 40 per cent of freights earned. Twenty seven voyages were made, with such cargoes as china clay, coal, grain, cement, manure and castings. The vessel ranged as far south as Brittany (before the fall of France), and the Cornish ports of Par and Charlestown.[121] The loss on the year's work was £1,097, and by that time the total accumulated loss had reached £2,258. By the time the preliminary results of the financial year 1940–41 became available it was clear that though a modest profit on the voyage account (£400) had been made, the vessel was not a great success; she was in fact too small. The contract with the Ardrossan Dockyard was accordingly cancelled on Christmas Day 1941, and on January 1942 it was reported that 'The majority of the shareholders being desirous of selling the vessel' it had been purchased on 10 January 1942 by Lovering & Sons Ltd, Cardiff, for £14,000 less 2½ per cent brokerage. Loverings operated her under the same name until 1951 when she passed into Norwegian hands.

By the time the *Kindiesel* was sold, the owners had become involved in agency work. Agency fees turned the accumulated loss for 1936–40 into a credit balance as at 30 September 1941, of £48. The *Kindiesel* experiment having come to an end, Kincaids sold their shareholding of 66 shares (including one transferred from James Scott Kincaid, who had died in 1940) to MacCallums (49 shares) and Hugh C Waterston, acting chairman of Mac-Callums (17 shares). Robert Greer's single share went to MacCallums. By

Table 6.7 *The Kindiesel Shipping Co. Ltd. Profit and Loss 1936–46*

	Trading profit and loss
	£
1936–7	−285
1937–8	−272
1938–9	−458
1939–40	−1,097
1940–1	400
1941–2	−665[1]
1942–3	464
1943–4	648
1944–5	2,083
1945–6	1,487

Source: *Managers' reports in Minute Book.*
[1] *Vessel sold 10 January 1942. Agency work 1942–6. Thereafter company assets mainly Government Securities.*
Note: *Financial Year 1 October–30 September.*

February 1943 the company was acting as agents for the *SS Strait Fisher* and the motor vessels *Ann M*, *David M*, and *Ngakoa*. The agency work allowed the organization of the shipping office to be maintained so that the company could 'take advantage of any favourable opportunity that may arise in respect of new tonnage'. In the meantime, the cash obtained by the sale of the *Kindiesel* was invested in Government securities. This enabled the company to give the Ministry of War Transport a bank guarantee of £15,000 as a condition of taking over the management of three vessels, the *Nordost*, *Margo* and *Ophir* from MacCallums on behalf of the Ministry. Agency and management fees boosted company profits from £464 in 1942–3 to £2,083 in 1944–5. By the time the 1944–5 results were available two of the four vessels which had been managed, the *Margo* and the *Nordost* had been returned to their owners, and a third, the *Ophir*, was on the point of being returned. The managers pointed out that it would be necessary to secure further management contracts if profits were not to drop.

In the post-war climate, management contracts were not easy to come by, and prices of new tonnage were high. The assets of the company continued, therefore, to be invested in Government securities, which were sold in 1948 at a profit. The capital cost of a new ship, however, remained prohibitive, and the company operated as a largely non-trading concern with a small amount of agency work until it was decided in 1962 to wind it up. The winding up was completed on 27 August, when a total of £26,241 was returned to the shareholders – a very reasonable return on an initial investment of £13,500.

A Maritime Postscript

Reflecting their maritime business interests, and the wonderful cruising waters of the Clyde and the West of Scotland, the Lang and Fulton families have included in successive generations a number of keen yachtsmen. An odd incident worth recording here was the use of a yacht formerly owned by James F Lang, the sloop *Gometra*, for a most unusual purpose. Charles Rawlings, writing in *Yachting* in February 1941 described how he found and identified her in 'an Eastern Canadian Port', where she had come as deck cargo on a small Norwegian steamer. On further investigation he discovered that she, and another Clyde-built yacht, the *Sinbad*, had been used to ship part of the Norwegian gold reserves to Canada as the Germans occupied the country. About half of the gold was evacuated by British cruiser, and the remainder had been loaded into the two yachts, which were towed up the Norwegian coast, where they were hoisted aboard the freighter. In the event of the vessel being sunk, it was reckoned that the yachts would have floated off.[122]

The sloop Gometra

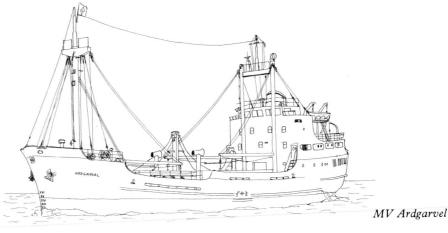

MV Ardgarvel

Chapter 7

Finished with Engines 1945–74

British industrialists did not regard the coming peace in 1945 with the same optimism as they had in 1918. They were not in a position to undertake massive capital investment, as wartime profits had been small, and most had only managed to recoup the losses of the depression years by the outbreak of war. The large debts to the United States incurred during the war required servicing and repayment, which would inevitably result in high levels of taxation and in weakness of sterling in relation to the hard currencies. Political uncertainty made forecasting even more difficult. The election of a Labour Government committed to a socialist Britain posed threats of nationalization to steel and shipbuilding. In the interim, Government controls introduced during the war were maintained by the Steel Distribution Scheme run by the Ministry of Supply, as there were acute shortages of steel throughout the world. Under these regulations, steel merchants acted purely as forwarding agents, selling at fixed prices and taking a standard commission.

The politicians who advocated nationalization agreed with the steelmasters in wishing to cut out the steel merchants from the home trade. Their objectives were, however, totally different. The politicians believed that if customers were dealing with a unitary supplier, with a standard pricing policy, the function of the merchant disappeared. The steelmasters, on the other hand, wished to 'assert and maintain their separate identity through direct contact with the users'.[2] Between 1945 and nationalization the masters gradually reduced their support of the merchants by cutting discounts on the Government prices to notional levels and then cancelling them altogether. This they were able to do as they were operating in a sellers' market, especially in MacCallums' traditional trade in ship steel.

Government policy combined with the steelmakers actions depressed MacCallums' returns. The domestic trade in merchant steel languished, but the export business resumed in 1945, and dominated the merchant department,[3] though even here problems were experienced with Government controls. The quotas of iron and steel for export were reported as being cut by 25 per cent for the early part of 1947, no doubt as a consequence of the acute fuel shortages of that bleak winter.[4] At the 41st General Meeting of the company in February 1949, it was reported that the export trade had increased during the financial year 1947–8, but that since 31 October 1948 competition from Belgium and Germany had developed, orders being lost to them on account of lower prices and quicker deliveries.[5] In March 1951 the comment was made that exports had declined 'due to lack of supplies available', and the shortages persisted throughout the year.[6] Although the bulk of MacCallums' export business was on a direct basis with their overseas customers, the company also maintained regular contact with many London merchant houses, such as the old-established firm of British steel exporters David Cameron & Co (London) Ltd, with whom an excellent business relationship existed for many years covering shipments mainly to the Far East and West Africa. Mr Donald Cameron, formerly a director of David Cameron & Co, recalled in 1981 with pleasure his connection with MacCallums during the difficult trading conditions of those post-war years.

The company's shipping business contributed most of the profit in the first two years after the war. With the coming of peace, freight rates rose swiftly, and the Government was quick to lift regulations from the shipping industry. At the end of the war the MacCallum fleet consisted of two ageing coasters, the *Ardgryfe* and the *Ardgantock*. By the end of 1945 the *Ardgantock* had been de-requisitioned by the Ministry of War Transport and was trading satisfactorily, while the *Ardgryfe*, under off-survey repairs, was on the point of de-requisitioning.[7] The profits from shipping in 1945 and 1946 totalled £19,292.[8] With the intention of investing in new tonnage, a reserve fund of £25,000 in government stock was created in April 1947. Profits from shipping peaked in 1946–7 at £22,358, and only slightly declined in the following year. During 1948–9, however, freight rates dropped by about a third, and heavy repair bills were incurred.[9]

Total profits (after allowing for a heavy tax burden) fell from £7,572 in 1944–5 to only £4,033 in 1946.[10] The results in 1946–7 were only marginally better, but between 1947 and 1950 the shipping income boosted profits to around £14,000 a year. Provision for taxation, unnecessary during the war owing to pre-war losses and non-provision for depreciation, dominated the performance of the company during the later 1940s, with provisions for taxes rising from £10,005 in 1945–6 to £41,049 in 1947–8, though there was a drop to £33,693 in 1948–9, and to £27,704 in 1949–50, in which year the chairman Ian M Lang 'referred to the high incidence of taxation which coupled with high costs made it impossible for companies to plough back sufficient profits to replace wasting assets within a reasonable period.'[11] There were no changes in the Board during the late 1940s, but provision for the continuing family ownership of MacCallums was made by the transfer in 1947 of 6,000 of Ian M Lang's shares to Margaret H Lang and a further 6,000 to a trust for Peter M Lang, at that time only seven. Two years later an additional 6,000 shares were transferred by Ian M Lang to Peter M Lang's trust.

By 1950 the character of the world seaborne trade was changing rapidly. Britain's position as the dominant shipowning nation was being eroded. Her staple bulk export trade in coal declined in the face of serious fuel shortages at home and the substitution of oil for coal. Shippers were adopting new cargo-handling techniques, even in the coastal trades, and there was a movement towards larger shipments. These factors led to a reduction in freight rates for smaller coastal vessels from 1947 to 1950. In an effort to overcome this problem agreement regarding freight co-operation in the coasting tramp industry was reached in 1950 through the Chamber of Shipping of the United Kingdom,[12] and this coupled with the outbreak of the Korean War, may have helped in a recovery in freight rates towards the end of the year. Profits on

MV Ardglen *in the dry dock of James Lamont & Co of* *Greenock*

MacCallums' voyage account rose slightly in 1950, to £11,183,[13] and seemed set to improve again in 1951. The better prospects encouraged the company to contract with James Lamont & Co, Port Glasgow, for the construction of 'a new vessel, yard number 377, at a price of £124,000'.[14] This vessel, the motor ship *Ardglen*, of 1044 gross tons, started her maiden voyage from Greenock to Newlyn, Cornwall, in ballast on 17 March 1953.[15] The order brought the possibility of depreciating before tax assessment, and though the operating surplus rose from £43,103 in 1949–50 to £67,334 in 1950–1, provision for tax only increased by about £3,000 after allowing £33,120 depreciation.[16] Unfortunately before the delivery of the *Ardglen* freight rates fell and steel shortages also hit net profitability.

The post-war Labour Government encountered serious financial difficulties in implementing their socialist programme. These, coupled with problems encountered in drafting legislation and issuing orders for implementation, delayed steel nationalization, which was not universally supported in the Cabinet. It was not until after the election of a new Labour government with a very small majority in 1950, that the Iron & Steel Corporation of Great Britain was set up as a holding company. The Corporation took over from the Iron & Steel Board the control of prices and commissions, but had a brief existence. In October 1951 the Conservatives returned to power, committed to the immediate denationalization of the industry. Pressing financial problems resulting partly from the Korean War, prevented action until May 1953. In the interim, however, controls were abolished, and as the

MV Ardglen *working through the ice in the Gabriel Straits in August 1954*

management of individual companies had remained virtually unchanged, the steel trade began to return to something like pre-war conditions.[17] For Mac-Callums this resulted in the purchase of 35,562 tons of steel in 1952.[18] Of this about two thirds was merchant steel, and most of the remainder was for stock. This level of purchases was maintained until 1958 when the Clyde shipbuilding and engineering industries began to suffer from changing patterns of demand and increasingly severe foreign competition. For example, closure of the Suez Canal after the crisis of 1956 created a market for 'very large crude carriers' in which the Clyde yards were unable to compete.

Table 7.1 Steel purchases and sales 1952–74 (to nearest ton)

Year	Scottish Works	English and Welsh Works	Total (inc. sundries)	Direct Sales	Stock	Export
1952	21,472	12,097	35,562	23,863	8,306	3,414
1953	18,433	12,446	33,545	21,768	9,795	1,981
1954	15,933	13,614	32,338	22,656	7,146	2,536
1955	15,642	9,565	26,917	17,623	8,424	871
1956	17,102	10,975	32,180	20,760	9,130	2,290
1957	19,744	13,021	35,125	22,936	11,009	1,958[1]
1958	13,557	11,297	31,335	25,107	4,514	1,714[2]
1959	9,865	6,992	18,152	14,306	3,725	121
1960	11,696	9,199	22,730	14,898	8,231	12
1961	12,299	11,671	26,098	19,102	6,756	241
1962	9,837	9,226	20,658	15,776	4,389	383
1963	7,022	7,559	16,756	12,303	4,281	182
1964	10,716	8,475	22,509	13,711	8,502	296
1965	6,767	9,653	19,499	10,808	8,304	388
1966	4,908	7,198	14,394	8,427	5,733	233
1967	3,298	7,334	12,856	6,520	6,146	191
1968	6,528	7,705	16,794	7,999	8,623	171
1969	8,722	8,046	19,965	7,794	12,106	65
1970	(a)		16,270	3,590	12,532	148
1971			7,927	2,296	5,502	129
1972			6,916	1,327	5,589	—
1973			9,917	830	9,086	—
1974			7,701	214	7,487	—

[1] Plus 4,063 tons imports.
[2] Includes 5,400 tons imported steel.
Notes (a) from 1970 tonnages were given by British Steel Corporation divisions.
        (b) from 1972 the original figures were in tonnes: the figures in the table are conversions.
Source: Calculated from PMS file Works Tonnages.

The recovery in the steel business was not paralleled on the shipping side. In 1953, the year of delivery of the *Ardglen*, a loss of £3,230 on the voyage account was recorded, the first since the war.[19] During the year, the *Ardglen* crossed the Atlantic in the late summer, and reached Chicago via the St Lawrence Seaway, reputedly the first British vessel to use it.[20] During November of the following year while on passage from Bathurst, New Brunswick, to Manchester she rescued four of the crew of MV *Tresillian* when she foundered during a force 12 gale in the St George's Channel. The Master, Captain F W McLaren, subsequently received a recommendation from the

Ministry of Transport and Civil Aviation in recognition of the work of himself and his crew.[21] He had an interesting career. He was born in India at Nagpur, and started his seagoing career with the British India Steam Navigation Co. He was for a time a member of the renowned Rangoon Pilot Service and then decided that he would like to work on small vessels. His association with MacCallums began when he shipped on the *Kindiesel* as mate, quickly rising to become master of that vessel. He then transferred to the *Ardgryfe* and was on board her in France when that country capitulated to the invading German forces. As first master of the *Ardglen* he enjoyed the challenge of operating in Canadian waters, where the vessel was on time charter for much of 1954 and 1955.[22]

The business proved rewarding with profits on the voyage account recovering to £6,548 in 1954. Early in 1955 the *Ardgantock* was sold to the Kyle Shipping Co, managed by Monroe Bros of Liverpool[23] and a second motorship, was ordered from James Lamont & Co, yard number 388, at a price of £175,000.[24] She was launched on 16 January 1957, and named *Ardgarry*. On delivery, in May 1957, she joined her near-sister on time

Captain F W McLaren receiving a reward for his work in rescuing the crew of MV Tresillian *in 1953*

Table 7.2 Extract from Abstract Log of MV Ardglen

Sailed from	Date	Arrived at	Date	Cargo
Greenock	17.3.53	Newlyn	19.3.53	Ballast[1]
Newlyn	20.3.53	Thames	20.3.53	Stone
Deptford	24.3.53	Billingham	26.3.53	Ballast
Billingham	28.3.53	Dublin	1.4.53	Bagged fertilizers
Dublin	2.4.53	Waterford	3.3.53	do.
Waterford	4.4.53	Cork	4.4.53	do.
Cork	4.4.53	Partington	6.4.53	Ballast
Partington	8.4.53	Cork	9.4.53	Coal
Cork	11.4.53	Newlyn	12.4.53	Ballast
Newlyn	13.4.53	London	15.4.53	Stone
London	16.4.53	Setubal	22.4.53	Coal
Setubal	24.4.53	Pomaron	26.4.53	Ballast
Pomaron	28.4.53	Dublin	4.5.53	Ore
Dublin	7.5.53	Barry	8.5.53	Ballast
Barry	9.5.53	Nantes	11.5.53	Coal
Nantes	12.5.53	Bordeaux	13.5.53	Ballast
Bordeaux	16.5.53	Newport	19.5.53	Pitwood
Barry	22.5.53	Leixoes	25.5.53	Coal
Leixoes	29.5.53	Port Talbot	2.6.53	Iron ore
Cardiff	12.6.53	Swansea	12.6.53	Steel
Swansea	15.6.53	Detroit	7.7.53	Steel
Detroit	8.7.53	Hamilton	9.7.53	Scrap
Hamilton	13.7.53	Montreal	18.7.53	Scrap
Montreal	18.7.53	Ardrossan	31.7.53	Scrap
Ardrossan	4.8.53	Greenock	4.8.53	Ballast

Source: *Abstract Log Book.*
[1] *Maiden voyage.*

charter in Canada,[25] where the *Ardglen* had been earning good freights, boosting profits on the voyage account to over £34,000 in both 1955 and 1956. After the boom years of the mid-1950s, shipping profits declined. On the voyage account these dropped to £25,532 in 1957 and slumped to £9,687 in 1958 and £7,587 in 1959.[26] At the end of the year the MacCallums' last steamship, the *Ardgryfe* was sold for £7,250 (less 2 per cent commission) to the British Iron & Steel Corporation (Salvage) Ltd. She was broken up by T W Ward at Preston.[27]

There was little change in the management of the company during the 1950s. In October 1954 John D Dempster decided to retire as a director, after an amazing 55 years service with MacCallums. He had been the mainstay of the company during the Second World War. Among his last duties was to visit Canada, where the *Ardglen* was trading, with a view to increasing business there.[28] Owing to the accumulation of a superannuation fund since 1944, MacCallums were able to give J D Dempster a pension commensurate with his long and valuable service. He was succeeded on the board in 1957 by Thomas D R Taylor, who had been with the company since 1917, having been manager of the Iron and Steel Department since 1954. J D Dempster's shares were transferred to trustees for Peter MacCallum Lang, to Hugh C Waterston, to Thomas D R Taylor and to the company secretary, Robert C

The launch of Ardgarry *from the Port Glasgow yard of James Lamont & Co in May 1957*

MV Ardgarry *at Grangemouth Docks shortly after her launch*

Clark, who had joined MacCallums in 1918 and was appointed secretary in 1954.

During the late 1950s the denationalized steel firms changed their selling policy by establishing their own network of agents, as supply overtook demand from their established customers. Steel merchants like MacCallums expanded their stockholding business and extended their ranges to include semi-finished steel products and bright drawn bars and dealing in scrap. MacCallums entered the scrap business buying back material from their customers. They also extended their established non-ferrous business. However, this was a volatile trade, dependent on fluctuations in the metal market. The years 1951 and 1957 were good with a total of 1,300 tons sold to Barr & Co (Brassfounders) Ltd, of which both Hugh C Waterston and Ian M Lang were in their turn directors. The main suppliers of this material were E Chalmers & Co Ltd, Leith, Park and Paterson Ltd, Glasgow, and A W Wanless & Co, Middlesbrough.[29]

With the onset of the depression in 1959 it became difficult for MacCallums to maintain their level of sales. The export market, never dominantly important, collapsed in the face of European competition and the merchant business dropped by about a third from the average level of the 1950s to about 15,000 tons and only recovered in the short-lived shipbuilding boom of 1961. Thereafter this business fell away, as the Clyde shipbuilding industry suffered traumatic contraction and reorganization.[30]

Up to 1951 Barclay, Curle & Co Ltd and Scott's were MacCallums' largest customers, but Barclay, Curle orders tailed off in 1952 and ended in 1954.[31] Smaller local yards – Lobnitz & Co, the Ardrossan Dockyard Ltd, George Brown & Co (Marine) Ltd, Ferguson Brothers (Port Glasgow) Ltd, and James Lamont & Co – remained faithful to MacCallums, though the size of their orders declined after the boom of the early 1950s. The severe recession in the shipbuilding industry in the early 1960s forced the liquidation of Ardrossan, and the amalgamation of Lobnitz with William Simons & Co in 1960, followed by the closure of the joint yard in 1965. George Brown & Co temporarily gave up shipbuilding. Finally, the integration of Ferguson Brothers and Scotts into the Lithgow dominated Scott-Lithgow group in 1967 ended old merchanting connections.

This decline was to a limited extent offset by expansion of non-shipbuilding custom: the largest consumer was James Howden & Co Ltd, who had first come to MacCallums in 1940.[32] The then managing director of Howdens, James Howden Hume, was a close personal friend of Ian M Lang.[33] The Howden connection was particularly important in the 1950s, when the firm was MacCallums' biggest customer for steel. The next largest was Kincaids, an old-established connection, with Davidson & Co Ltd of Belfast third. The other consumers, although they made much smaller demands, were an interesting group, including James Mackie & Co, the Belfast textile machinery manufacturers. The Belfast trade was killed by the high cost of freight, and by competition with stockholders established there in the early 1960s,[34] while the integration of Kincaids into the Scott-Lithgow group in 1967 ended merchant orders from that source.

In common with their competitors MacCallums found that the scale and profitability of merchant business were so low that they were forced to fall back on their original business of stockholding. This dated back to the origins of the company in the eighteenth century, but for much of the intervening period had been overshadowed by shipowning or merchanting. John Macdonald, the director in charge of the stockholding side of MacCallums in 1981, recalled the use, until about 1950, of horse lorries and hand carts for deliveries in Greenock, with traction engines to bring steel from the harbour. The Cappielow yard was fitted with foundry-type hand cranes. Bar steel up to six inches in diameter was sawn by hand with a hacksaw, and the men used to send out for onions to lubricate the blade. The Rue End Street covered store had an overhead crane with timber frame running on wooden rails, and the steel was stored in vertical racks on either side of a central walkway. These primitive conditions were typical of many iron and steel stockholders at that time.[35] An old-established part of this business was the West Highland trade with local blacksmiths, who were served by MacBrayne's cargo steamers direct from Greenock. These men relied on MacCallums, not only to supply them with iron and steel, but also with a range of other products,

An advertisement for MacCallums' stock steel, 1965

including tools. Though this trade has now declined, the firm of George Currie & Sons of Sandbank, founded in 1851, has survived to claim that it is MacCallums' oldest customer.[36] Another significant West Highland trade was that in Department of Agriculture corrugated iron sheets, but this collapsed in the mid-1950s when the Department instituted central buying. MacCallums, however, still supply steel to the Outer Isles.[37]

Records of the stockholding side of MacCallum's business after the Second World War are scanty, the evidence available suggests the volume of trade increased fairly steadily from 1948. It was concerned largely with shipbuilding material. The year 1944–5 was a 'good average year' with the new stockyard at Mackenzie Street (acquired at the end of the war) 'proving

Table 7.3 Peter MacCallum & Sons Ltd – Profits and
Taxation Provision 1945–60
(Financial Year 1 November–31 October)

Year	Net Profit	Provision for Taxation
1945–6	4,033	10,005
1946–7	6,504	30,878
1947–8	14,796	41,049
1948–9	13,813	33,693
1949–50	15,399	27,704
1950–1	3,429	30,785
1951–2	13,935	31,514
1952–3	6,046	29,015
1953–4	7,329	21,196
1954–5	12,031	47,125
1955–6	16,889	70,223
1956–7	1,527	41,234
1957–8	7,368	14,940
1958–9	8,674	13,260
1959–60	47,573	38,468

Source: Directors' reports in Minute Books

a most valuable asset'.[38] During 1946–7 there was increased turnover in the Steel Department with 'exceptional demand for supplies from stock'.[39] and this general profitability continued to the end of 1952, when it was proposed to erect a new sheet store at Mackenzie Street.[40] The decision taken in February 1953 not to go ahead with this proposal suggests that there might have been a recession, but by 1954–5 there was again 'increased turnover' in the stock department, which continued through the following year.[41] The three years for which figures exist, 1958–9, 1959–60 and 1960–1 show sales rising from £205,354 to £407,120 then dropping to £351,413. Profits behaved in the same way, grossing £28,484, and £20,804.[42] In 1959–60 this represented a profit on turnover of just over 11 per cent, as compared with 0.8 per cent on merchant activities in the same year. This seems to have been a peak year, but after a lull in the early 1960s activity in the iron and steel department resumed its upward trend. Gross profit for the year 1964–5 was

£52,854, most of which was presumably contributed by the stockholding business.[43] In 1969 a piece of ground adjacent to the Cappillow stockyard was purchased and a new warehouse with overhead cranage built for the storage of light bars and sections, at a total cost of about £30,000.[44]

In 1967 the nascent scrap business became potentially more important with the reaching of an agreement after nearly two years of discussion between MacCallums and the Greenock scrap-dealing firm Beveridge & Co about an amalgamation of their interests.[45] The immediate stimulus was the intention of British Railways to withdraw services from Greenock Albert Harbour and Knowe Road siding, offering instead the Garden siding on the Port Glasgow Harbour branch. This was totally unsuitable for the Greenock traders, and as a compromise the use of the Baker Street siding was agreed. The British Railways representatives preferred dealing with one customer, hence a merger on a 50/50 basis was agreed. The name chosen for the combine was Beveridge & Co Metals Ltd, on account of Beveridge & Co having been in business since 1887 and because they had built up 'a considerable reputation for fair dealing in a trade, which is open to many abuses'. Apart from simplifying dealings with British Railways the combination opened up the possibilities of introducing mechanical processing and handling. From MacCallums' point of view the merger reduced the workload on the staff, as the management of the scrap business was placed in the hands of the combine. The MacCallums scrap business was in both ferrous and non-ferrous metal, drawn from companies like Scotts', Kincaids' and Hasties'. The ferrous scrap went to Colvilles, Caledonian Foundry (which by that time belonged to Hasties'), Clyde Alloy, North British Steel Foundry and a number of smaller users. Non-ferrous went mainly to Park & Paterson Ltd, with smaller quantities to P & W MacLellan Ltd, R M Easdale & Co Ltd and John Allan (Glenpark) Ltd.[46]

The Shipping Department enjoyed fair trading conditions in the early 1960s with the profit on the voyage account rising to £26,300 in 1960, falling to £15,589 in 1961 and rising again to £24,669 in 1962.[47] Both vessels continued to spend the summer months in time charter in Canada. Tragically, however, immediately after her return from Canada the *Ardgarry* was lost with all twelve members of crew after sailing from Swansea on 28 December 1962 with coal for Rouen.[48] She was seen by the coastguard station at the Lizard on 29 December, with the wind blowing at force 7 to 8. During the evening the weather got worse, with easterly winds of force 9 to 11. The *Ardgarry* overtook a Dutch coaster, the *Hollandia*, and then suddenly appeared to alter course through 90 degrees to port right across the course of the *Hollandia*. At the same time she sent an SOS signal to the *Hollandia*. At that moment the masthead lights of the *Ardgarry* were seen to fall to the water on the starboard side. The inquiry into her loss, held at Swansea in October 1963, came to the view that the probable sequence of events was '(1) a sudden breakdown of the steering or of the engines or to the propeller falling off or striking a submerged object leading to (2) broaching to, resulting in loss of control and (3) a violent blow from a heavy breaker or breakers when the vessel was broadside on to the wind and sea causing a shift of cargoes at the last and consequently capsizing.' Absolving MacCallums from blame, the Wreck Commissioner commented that the *Ardgarry* had been very well maintained. Damaged lifeboats were recovered on the Scilly Isles and in Cornwall on January 4 and 5, but no trace of the crew was ever found. Immediately after results of the inquiry had been announced MacCallums indicated that they were considering a replacement vessel,[49] and on 15 October 1963 a contract was signed with Lamonts for a new motor vessel, yard number 402, at a fixed price of £206,000 for delivery on 31 October 1964.[50] Named *Ardgarvel*, she was not delivered until 28 January 1965, when

Table 7.4 *Shipping Account 1945–75*

Year	Profit on voyage Account	Depreciation	Net Profit	Valuation	Index of Real Freights
1945	—	—	7,753	3,000	—
1946	—	—	11,539	3,000	—
1947	—	—	22,358	3,000	—
1948	24,876	—	21,270	3,000	—
1949	9,010	—	12,010	3,000	—
1950	11,183	—	11,683	3,000	—
1951	18,077	33,120	15,077	52,680	—
1952	16,641	51,550	13,642	80,327	100
1953	−3,230	66,246	20	83,000	74
1954	6,548	76,934	9,298	74,000	79
1955	34,509	130,934	21,009	120,000	110
1956	34,719	155,170	24,719	172,500	125
1957	25,532	166,320	25,532	180,000	84
1958	9,687	174,076	9,687	173,000	50
1959	7,587	187,491	7,587	160,000	51
1960	26,300	226,005	26,300	120,000	53
1961	15,589	237,685	20,089	110,000	—
1962	24,669	253,020	20,305	95,000	—
1963	13,495	205,860	14,002	15,000	—
1964	3,712	218,238	3,946	110,000	—
1965	16,740	238,938	17,095	135,000	—
1966	13,115	263,938	13,306	110,000	—
1967	−2,462	274,865	−2,446	100,000	—
1968	6,397	286,583	6,432	90,000	—
1969	17,702	307,773	17,909	72,000	—
1970	5,545	324,687	5,726	52,000	—
1971	−20,782	336,637	−20,517	43,000	—
1972	16,328	177,481[1]	16,530	35,500	—
1973	−7,097	182,981	−8,001	30,000	—
1974	−10,153	187,830	9,211	28,000	—
1975	−21,793	—[2]	20,805	—	—

[1] *1972 adjusted for sale of* Ardglen.
[2] *1975 adjusted for sale of* Ardgarvel.
Sources: *Company Accounts. Years given are financial years, i.e. 1945 is 1 November 1944 to 31 October 1945. Note that the depreciation figures are cumulative. In 1963 £68,365, being the amount realized during the year over Book Value was written off the value of shipping property.*

The Index of Real Freights is from S G Sturmey, British Shipping and World Competition, *1962, table 27 on p. 179.*

she began trading with coal between Ayr and East Yelland, Devon.[51] She had an uneventful career until 30 October 1968, when she went aground on rocks near San Sebastian, Spain.[52] The vessel was in ballast on her way from Bilbao to Pasajes in perfect visibility and weather conditions when the master of the vessel, who was navigating by radar, fell asleep. The *Ardgarvel* was towed off by two French tugs, and repaired at a reported cost of about £28,000. The Master, whose previous career had been blameless, had his master's foreign-going certificate suspended for a year. A curious feature of the incident was that the SOS call was picked up by the piermaster at Kilcreggan on the Clyde, 900 miles away. The *Ardgarvel* also attracted publicity in 1972 when she had as a crew member an eighteen year old girl from Holywell in North Wales.[53] Before 'equal opportunities' this was daring indeed.

The launch of MV Ardgarvel *from James Lamont's yard in 1965 by Mrs Brenda Fulton (widow of J V Fulton), and a spectacular view of the vessel ashore near San Sebastian in Spain in 1968*

After 1962 profits on the voyage account became uncertain, dipping to a loss of nearly £2,500 in 1967, but with good years in 1965 and 1969, when profits amounted to about £17,000.[54] These results coupled with the uneasy fortunes of the metal trade were reflected in the profit and loss account. Early in 1961 two directors died within five weeks. Thomas D R Taylor died on 6 February, and Hugh C Waterston on 11 March. Thomas Taylor had been with the company for 44 years, and had been a director since 1957. He was greatly missed.[55] Hugh Crawford Waterston had joined the board at the beginning of the Second World War when his nephews, James V and Robert W Fulton had been called up on active service and became a trustee for James's children. As Vice Chairman and Managing Director of Bairds and Scottish Steel Ltd, his experience of the steel trade was extensive, and of great value to MacCallums. He had latterly been a director of William Baird & Co, John Hastie & Co, the Caledonian Foundry Ltd, and was from 1952 a

*Hugh C Waterston, a director of P MacCallum & Sons
and chairman of Bairds and Scottish Steel Ltd*

trustee of the Clyde Navigation Trust. He retired most of his directorships
in 1960, but remained with MacCallums until his death at the age of eighty-
five.[56] Mr Taylor was replaced on the board by the company secretary,
Robert C Clark. Mr Clark was in turn succeeded by Walter P McLean, who
had been with the company since 1937. Mr Taylor's shares were transferred
to Mr Clark and Mr MacLean. Mr Waterston's place as a director was taken
by James F Lang. During the early 1960s a series of share transfers took place
which concentrated holdings in the hands of the children of James F and Ian
M Lang. Early in 1964, Walter P McLean, was elected a director. John D
Dempster died, having been retired for ten years. His shareholding was
acquired by Walter McLean and by members of the Lang and Fulton families, in equal quantities. In October 1965 Peter M Lang's trustees handed
over the MacCallums shareholdings to him. He was elected a director at the
fifty-ninth Ordinary General Meeting of the company on 2nd March 1967.
Peter Lang represents the eighth generation of Langs in MacCallums. Robert
I Clark retired in July 1969 after 51 years service, and his place on the board
was taken in 1971 by Robin L V Fulton, son of James V Fulton, who had
succeeded to the shares held in trust for him in March 1970. At the same
time John Macdonald was also elected a director.

During 1967 the British steel industry was renationalized by the Labour Government. The structure of the industry was completely altered, and the old firms submerged in new product-based divisions. As a consequence, the new British Steel Corporation stopped supplying merchants, preferring to use their own selling agencies.[57] Despite prolonged attempts by the Steel Distributors Association to reach agreement with the British Steel Corporation, that organization proved 'unshakably anti-merchant'. As a result the Steel Distributors Association was wound up and the capital returned to the members. For MacCallums this meant the end of old connections and confirmed the return of the business to its original trade of stockholding, with some merchant steel being bought from the few surviving independent steel companies. Curiously, the volume of merchant business increased slightly after nationalization though it declined sharply after 1972. The stockholding business showed similar trends to 1972 but recovered thereafter. No details are available for the steel side of the business after 1974, but MacCallums have continued to specialize in the supply of shipbuilding steel of quality to their established customers. In addition they are developing a trade in general and other specialized steels with new consumers engaged in advanced industries.

The shipping side of the business encountered similar difficulties due, not to nationalization, but to the rationalization of the British shipping industry into a number of powerful groups. These were formed because the cost of ships was rising quickly at the same time as the industry was being transformed by containerization. The traditional coasting trade was also subject to competition from family-owned continental vessels with their characteristically low overheads. MacCallums attempted to break out of this situation by developing a 'working association' with the old-established firm of John Stewart & Co (Shipping) Ltd, involving R L V Fulton, son of James V Fulton, and G E W Macfarlane of Stewarts. Agreement was eventually reached in April 1971 to link them by a chartering arrangement. Stewarts were authorized to do all the fixing of MacCallums' vessels and R L V Fulton was based at the Stewart office, where he was jointly responsible for chartering, and was charged with exploring possible joint ventures in new and specialized shipping.[59] Of these the most promising seemed to be vessels for the movement of heavy lifts. The agreement with Stewarts, however, only lasted for a year, being terminated on 25 April 1972, as R L V Fulton had to return to Greenock to replace Walter McLean as company secretary, who had died suddenly.

By that time MacCallums had decided to sell the *Ardglen*, which was nearly twenty years old. She went to the Hortiatis Shipping Co, Famagusta, Cyprus on 22 March 1972 for £28,250 less 7 per cent commission.[66] It was intended that she should be replaced by a vessel of about 3,200 tons deadweight, taking advantage of the depreciation allowances against taxation introduced by the Conservative Government in October 1970. However, quotations taken in the spring of 1974 indicated that the cost would be in excess of £1,250,000, which seemed prohibitive in view of the projected cash flow.[67] In August 1974 it was reported that the remaining vessel, the *Ardgarvel*, was having continuing trouble with her propelling machinery, with large main engine parts having to be replaced regularly. Two pistons required replacement in July, and extensive tailshaft repairs were necessary. The company was also having problems in recruiting crews and the vessel was regularly sailing short-handed. Even though salaries well above recommended rates were being paid, it was found difficult both to recruit and retain crew members. The report of the Shipping Department also noted that 'there has been a marked decline in the standard of Ships' Officers and Deck Crew so much so that we are of the opinion that British Short Sea Owners will have an ever increasing difficulty in satisfactorily manning their vessels.'[62] The disadvantages of running a single ship were also becoming apparent. The only way the board could see to produce additional revenue was to put her in the hands of a 'first-class management company', which would cost an additional £7,000 per annum.[63] During 1974 the world went into deep recession following the dramatic rise in oil prices as a consequence of the October war of the previous year. Charter rates for shipping dropped by two thirds in the first six months of the year. As the outlook was so bleak MacCallums resolved to put the *Ardgarvel* on the market as soon after 1 November 1974 as possible, ending direct shipowning interests of Mac-Callums after fifty four years, and of the Lang and Fulton families after about 100 years. The *Ardgarvel* was sold on 28 November 1974 to Henry W Peabody Grain Ltd, London, for £245,000 less 1 per cent commission, and renamed *Balmerino*.[64] In 1977 Peabodys in turn sold her 'to unnamed interests' for about £250,000.

By the end of 1974 MacCallums was at a crossroads. The company could either distribute their surplus assets, principally the ship replacement fund, to their shareholders, or they could seek new investment opportunities. The distribution of funds, as in 1927, was now no longer sensible as a large tax liability would have been incurred. The new generation of directors, Peter Lang and Robin Fulton, had to take the lead as Ian M Lang became ill and was forced to withdraw gradually from the business. In the very difficult trading conditions of the mid-1970s their choice was hard. As a first step in an effort to win new stockholding business, particularly from overseas customers they decided to modernize and enlarge the Mackenzie steel warehouse at a cost of £28,000.[65]

In comparison with the violent fluctuations in fortune characteristic of the period between 1920 and 1939, the post-war years had been remarkably free from trauma for MacCallums as a company. The commitment of successive post-war governments to expansionist policies ensured that such changes as did take place were gradual, though the long-term effects of these movements were very considerable. In particular the social and economic programme pursued by post-war governments threatened the existence of a company like MacCallums. Not only were taxes imposed on profits at a level higher than ever before in peacetime, but the pricing agreements arrived at in self-defence through trade associations were made illegal, and changes in the Companies Acts made the conduct of business much more public, and therefore substantially reduced freedom of manœuvre. These unpublicized constraints on operation certainly had a more profound effect on the company than the nationalization and denationalization of steel. Perhaps the most profound effect of government economic thinking was, however, the equation of the traditional industries of steel, shipbuilding and heavy engineering with decline, 'progress' resting on new, light industries.

Chapter 8

Security for the Future 1974–1982

During the early 1970s most British shipping companies diversified into other activities. In Scotland, for example, the Lyle Shipping Company and Hogarth & Sons Ltd became deeply involved in the supply and servicing of the North Sea Oil industry.[1] Some shipping concerns abandoned shipowning altogether, becoming ship managers or brokers or investing in related industries. The directors of MacCallums chose in the short run to diversify away from shipowning and operation. The board, led by Peter Lang and Robin Fulton, therefore looked for suitable investment opportunities.

The first fruit of this policy was the acquisition in April 1975 of offices and ground at the south west corner of Baker Street and Scott Street, Greenock.[2] This property had originally belonged to Rankin & Blackmore, marine engineers, who ceased trading in the early 1960s. The offices, renamed Mac-Callum House, were more modern and spacious than those in Rue End Street, which were demolished in the spring of 1976 and the site sold.[3] The move away from the dock area in a way symbolized the change in the company away from direct involvement in marine affairs, though MacCallums still acted as agents for vessels visiting the Clyde.

At the same time the decision was taken to acquire the engineering business of Cochranes (Bo'ness) Ltd of Seaview Works, Bo'ness, on the south shore of the River Forth.[4] This gave the MacCallums a physical presence on the east coast of Scotland at a time when the Government was giving every encouragement to Scottish businesses to become involved in the expanding North Sea Oil industry. Cochranes was founded in 1861 by John Cochrane, a blacksmith.[5] The firm developed a trade in ship forgings, and must have benefited from the reconstruction of Bo'ness Harbour by the

114

Bo'ness Harbour, photographed in the early 1890s, with ships loading coal and paddle steam tugs standing by

A group photograph of the members of the United General Sea Box of Borrowstouness (Bo'ness), a friendly society founded in 1634. John Cochrane, the founder of Cochranes, seated at the far left

North British Railway in the 1880s, which stimulated an export trade in coal and imports of timber, especially pit props. By 1878 John Cochrane was also described as an engineer, and was kept busy with general repair work for the industries of the area, including the local foundries, the Linlithgow paper mills and Hurll's fireclay works at Manuel. As can be seen from his photograph, John Cochrane was a fine figure of a man, and he played an important role in the affairs of the town. Among other activities he was a member of the United General Sea Box of Borrowstouness Friendly Society, founded in 1634, one of the oldest organizations of its kind in Scotland. He had nine sons, four of whom followed him into the business. The eldest, John F Cochrane, was born in 1882, and served his time as an engineer, moving to South Africa, where he took charge of an engineering works. On the death of his father, he returned to Bo'ness to take charge of Cochranes, which was then styled John Cochrane jun. By 1912 the other brothers had been taken into the firm which took out limited liability in that year, becoming Cochrane Brothers Ltd.[6] During the First World War the company employed about a hundred blacksmiths making horse-shoes for the British Army. The company also carried out joiner work for the building trades, and in the 1920s was involved in the building of a number of cinemas as well as speculative housing. This side of the business collapsed about 1932 as a result of the depression. The firm maintained a brass foundry (latterly specializing in modern bearing materials) until 1969. James (Jimmy) took charge of the repair works operated by the company at Grangemouth Docks, but on his death, just before the Second World War, this branch was closed. Dan fought in the First World War, losing a hand at Beaumont Hamel. On his return he took over the management of the company's transport fleet, building it up as a general carrier. Traffic handled by the fleet, which at its maximum consisted of nine or ten lorries, included timber imports, flour from the Scottish Co-operative Wholesale Society's Chancelot Mills in Leith, and castings from the local foundries. When the nationalized British Road Services was set up in 1948, Dan became area manager. He returned to Cochranes in 1960 when British Road Service's management structure was reorganized. He died on 31 December 1973. The remaining brother, Tom, was a time-served pattern-maker, and became a director of the company. During the Second World War the company controlled Bo'ness Docks, where they made modifications to tank landing craft. Immediately after the war they were involved in the conversion of minesweepers back to trawlers.

John F Cochrane, like his father, took an active interest in Bo'ness affairs. He was for a time chairman of Bo'ness Football Club, which gained First Division status in 1929, but had to close in 1934 as a consequence of the depression. Cochranes built the stand, and when the club closed, Mr Cochrane handed over the deeds to the Town Council. The ground is now the base for Bo'ness United, an active and successful junior club. He was also a Justice of the Peace, and in the light of his obvious energy it is not surprising that he continued work until he was well into his seventies. He died in 1970.

By that time effective control of the company, which had been reconstructed in 1932 as Cochranes (Bo'ness) Ltd[7] was in the hands of William (Bill) Cochrane. Though the earliest specialities of the company, blacksmithing, shipsmithing, and ship repairing had become greatly reduced in importance as a consequence of the closure of the docks, it had developed the repair and maintenance side of the business, continuing its close connection with local concerns, which by then included the Grangemouth oil refinery and petrochemical complex. To meet changing needs, the company had diversified into welded fabrication. Bill Cochrane was, however, finding the running of the business a strain, and in 1975 welcomed the opportunity to become involved with MacCallums. Peter M Lang and Robin L V Fulton became directors of the company and the latter soon moved to the East Coast to take over the full-time running of the business. In making this investment decision MacCallums were conscious of the importance of the connections with the Grangemouth oil-refining complex, and of the possibilities of involvement with the North Sea Oil work. To cope with changing conditions, entirely new offices and workshops were built in 1979 to replace some of the older buildings on the site.[8] The company, apart from continuing to produce fabricated steel work for a wide range of customers, also undertakes mechanical maintenance contracts.

In 1976 the MacCallum board was strengthened to help with these new commitments by the appointment of Ian Bruce Lang,[9] who had followed his father James F Lang into insurance broking. He had also maintained the link

The shop floor of Cochranes in 1981, showing various prefabrication jobs in progress

117

of the previous three generations with the savings bank movement, becoming a Trustee of the West of Scotland Trustee Savings Bank. In May 1979 he was elected to Parliament to represent Galloway, and in 1981 he joined the Government as the Scottish Government Whip. As a result he had to give up his directorship of MacCallums, but remains a shareholder. During 1977 Peter Lang took over as chairman of the company in succession to his father Ian M Lang who after forty years in the chair was now forced to retire owing to continuing ill-health.

In 1981 MacCallums took the bold decision to enter an entirely new area of business when they acquired from the receiver the whole of the fixed trading assets of Thomas Brands and Sons Ltd, a Greenock company formed in 1971.[10] This concern's original activities were electrical engineering and contracting and armature winding. In 1979 it developed a specialization in intruder alarms and industrial monitoring, but rapid growth had created a cash-flow problem. With the resources of MacCallums behind it, Brands is already developing new types of security systems to exploit a quickly ex-

The board of P MacCallum & Sons in 1981. From left to right Robin Fulton, James Fulton Lang, Peter MacCallum Lang, Ian Bruce Lang and John McDonald

118

A display of Brands' services at an exhibition in 1982

panding market. Although the electrical contracting and armature winding divisions were important in the acquisition it was the potential of the security division which held the main attraction for MacCallums. This division bases its operations from a continuously manned Central Control Room into which are fed intruder alarms and industrial monitoring devices. Industrial monitoring takes the form of: for example, the continuous surveillance of boiler-house controls at a factory in Paisley, the continuous oversight of deep freezes in a supermarket in Edinburgh. It obviates the necessity for a full-time watchman where there is any form of continuous process, thereby saving the employers considerable sums in wages and, possibly, in loss of production. Closed circuit television and security fencing are other specialities of Brands, who using these techniques, have also more recently researched and developed an entirely new security system for fish farm cages.

During 1981 Brands' Alarms qualified for election as members of the National Security Council of Intruder Alarms which effectively recognized the high quality of workmanship carried out by the company on its installations.

While these new ventures were being launched, the new generation did not neglect the firm's original stockholding trade. The new offices gave the company a modern image which underpinned the directors' efforts to find new customers. Between 1974 and 1979 the McKenzie Street warehouses were extended, new cranage was installed both inside and outside, and neighbouring ground was acquired for future expansion.[11] Although the trade dipped in the mid-1970s recession, it recovered well in the later years of the decade, and MacCallums remain one of the few truly independent Scottish steel stockholders.

As these foundations for the future were being built up, Ian MacCallum Lang died after a long illness in November 1981. He had been a director of John Hastie & Co and of the Caledonian and Barr's foundries. Following in the family tradition, he had been a director of the Greenock Provident Bank, and was associated with the Mariners' Home and Greenock Medical Aid Society. He was also a Justice of the Peace. Speaking at his funeral service on 5 November, the Reverend David Mill, of Finnart – St Paul's Church – referred to the patient way in which he had borne his illness, and commented

Ian MacCallum Lang

on his generous support of charitable causes and his church 'always quietly and discreetly', summing him up as 'a truly exceptional man, a truly great man, a truly good man'.

By becoming a group, with a balanced range of activities, MacCallums has shown the ability to adapt to changing conditions which has characterized it throughout its two hundred year history. Small businesses can take comfort from the history of MacCallums since 1781, as they face the uncertain trading conditions of the 1980s. Survival has always been more important than growth and the size of the firm coupled with continuous family control has given it the flexibility to respond quickly to the rises and falls of the economy.

Born in the Greenock of James Watt, raised on the Clyde of Bell and

Napier, it has played its part in the stories of such firms as Lithgows, Colvilles and Workman Clark. It survives today to bear witness to the prudence, the industry and the enterprise of countless hundreds of small companies that came and went over the two centuries it now celebrates, and the integrity and dedication of the generations of families who ran them. It has weathered the storms of industrial revolutions and wars and the more damaging assaults of taxation, nationalization and government interference that have destroyed so many companies over the years. Its story is surely worth telling.

References

Chapter 2
References

1. Daniel Weir, *History of Greenock* (1829), p. 89.
2. Extract from the MacCallum family bible in possession of Peter M Lang.
3. Glasgow University Archives (GUA) GD319/7/21, Greenock Foundry journals, 1803-5, pp. 95-6.
4. Greenock Statutory Register of Shipping, 1803.
5. Daniel Weir, *op. cit.*, p. 42.
6. *Ibid.*, p. 43, and L Cope Carnford, *Aberdeen Line 1825-1925* (1925), p. 22.
7. John Orbell, *From Cape to Cape: The History of Lyle Shipping Company* (1978), p. 14.
8. Daniel Weir, *op. cit.*, p. 90.
9. *Renfrew Sasines 1781-1820*, No. 10377.
10. *Ibid.*, Nos. 11394, 13736, and, *Renfrew Sasines 1821-1830*, No. 2387.
11. Notes on the history of the firm in the possession of P MacCallum & Sons Ltd and GUA, UGD153/13/2, stock book of D McLellan, 1830-32.
12. Scottish Record Office (SRO) CS96/3618, sequestration papers of Ewing Miller & Co and of Miller Fergus & Co, 1820, and, CS96/920/1, sequestration papers of Norman McLeod, 1828-9.
13. Greenock Statutory Register of Shipping, 1814 and 1818.
14. SRO, GD260/7/69. Miscellaneous records of D McIntosh, solicitor, Dumbarton.
15. Kenneth Warren, *Early Steel Sheet Industry* (1970), p. 21.
16. SRO, GD260/7/82. Miscellaneous records, etc., *op. cit.*
17. *Renfrew Sasines 1831-1840*, No. 2154.
18. Michael S Moss and John R Hume, *Workshop of the British Empire* (1977), pp. 87-8.
19. Gerald Graham, 'The Ascendancy of the Sailing Ship, 1850-85', *Economic History Review*, Vol. IX, No. 1, pp. 74-88.
20. Moss and Hume, *op. cit.*, pp. 93-4.
21. The records of William Denny Bros in GUA make no reference to the firm in the 1840s.
22. SRO, CS96/555, sequestration papers of James McMillan, 1843.
23. SRO, SC58/42/40, fol. 642-55, trust deed and inventory of Peter MacCallum, Greenock, 1854.
24. GUA, GD319/3/1, Scott & Co journal, 1857-64, *passim*.
25. SRO, SC58/42/30, fol. 125-8, inventory of James MacCallum, iron merchant, Greenock, 1861.

26. *Ibid.*
27. Sequestration papers of Peter MacCallum in possession of the firm, and, Ontario Archives, R622, Wentworth, insolvency docket book, 1868-80.
28. *Renfrew Sasines 1861-1864*, No. 280.
29. *Renfrew Sasines 1865-1868*, No. 1553.
30. *Ibid.*, No. 5397.
31. GUA, extracts from the Diaries and papers of Joseph Russell, 1834-1917, p. 13, and, *Edinburgh Gazette*, 1868.
32. SRO, SC58/42/38, fol. 449-52, inventory of Thomas Park MacCallum, 1869.
33. SRO, SC58/42/42, fol. 1110, inventory of Daniel MacCallum, 1874.
34. *Ibid.*
35. Notes on history of the firm, *op. cit.*

Chapter 3
References

1. SRO, CH2/97/6, Dumbarton Kirk Session minute book, 18 January 1805, p. 343.
2. General Register House, Edinburgh, OPR494/2, Cardross register of marriages, 6 April 1805.
3. SRO, SC65/34/6, inventory of James Lang, 27 June 1850, and, the family bible in possession of Peter M Lang.
4. *Dunbartonshire Sasines*, 13 August 1780, B16/2/8.
5. *Ibid.*, 5 March 1790, B16/2/9.
6. Donald MacLeod, *The God's Acres of Dumbarton* (1888), p. 232.
7. *Dunbartonshire Sasines*, 20 September 1783, B16/2/8, p. 1, and, 24 May 1805, B16/2/9.
8. David Lyon, *Denny List I* (1975), introduction.
9. *Dunbartonshire Sasines*, 13 February 1783, B16/2/8, and, 9 July 1810, B16/4/1.
10. SRO, RO4/286, bond by John Lang and his cautioner for payment of composition, 24 July 1809.
11. *Ibid.*
12. Donald Macleod, *The God's Acre of Dumbarton*, p. 230.
13. Michael S Moss and John R Hume, *Workshop of the British Empire* (1977), p. 86.
14. Donald Macleod, *Town and Castle of Dumbarton* (1877), pp. 194-5.
15. *Ibid.*, pp. 195-6.
16. SRO, CS271/58588, bill of advocation for James Lang v. Magistrates and Town Council of Dumbarton, 1811.
17. Donald Macleod, *Town and Castle of Dumbarton, op. cit.*, p. 188.
18. James Williamson, *Clyde Passenger Steamers from 1812-1901* (1904), pp. 44-9.
19. James Cleland, *Enumeration of the Inhabitants of the City of Glasgow* (1832), p. 159.
20. *Dunbartonshire Sasines*, 10 May 1823, m. 298.
21. *Ibid.*, 28 December 1827, B16/4/1.
22. Donald Macleod, *The God's Acre of Dumbarton, op. cit.*, pp. 247-8.
23. Scottish Record Society, *Roll of Dumbarton Burgesses and Guild Brethren 1600-1846* (1937).
24. Dumbarton Public Library (DPL), 7/6/1, sederunt book of the *Duke of Wellington*, meeting 15 May 1823.
25. *Ibid.*, contract of agreement.
26. *Ibid.*, *loc. cit.*
27. Sir James D Marwick, *The River Clyde and Clyde Burghs* (1909), pp. 199-202.
28. DPL 7/6/2, minute book of Dumbarton Steamboat Co, 12 March 1833, duties of steward.
29. *Ibid.*, meeting of 10 August 1826.
30. See, for example, Public Record Office (PRO), BT98/265, crew list of the *Dunoon Castle*, 1835.
31. DPL 7/6/2, *op. cit.*, meeting of 10 August 1826.
32. *Ibid.*, meetings of 5 February and 7 August 1828.
33. Donald Macleod, *History of Loch Lomond Steamboat Companies* (1889), p. 53.
34. *Ibid.*, pp. 41-6.
35. Donald Macleod, *The God's Acre of Dumbarton, op. cit.*, p. 232.
36. Donald Macleod, *History of Loch Lomond Steamboat Companies, op. cit.*, pp. 46 and 52-3.
37. DPL 7/6/2, *op. cit.*, meeting of 20 March 1828.
38. *Ibid.*, *passim.*

39. Calculated from quarterly accounts abstracted from DPL 7/6/2, *op. cit.*
40. DPL 7/6/2, *op. cit.*, meetings of 27 April 1830.
41. *Ibid.*, meetings of 17 June and 2 July 1830.
42. *Ibid.*, meeting of 6 May 1830.
43. *Ibid.*, meeting of 27 June 1834.
44. *Ibid.*, meeting of 3 March 1834.
45. Moss and Hume, *op. cit.*, pp. 87–8.
46. SRO, CS96/772/12, sequestration papers of John Lang, 1835–41.
47. *Renfrewshire Sasines*, 23 May 1837, No. 3909.
48. Donald Macleod, *The God's Acre of Dumbarton, op. cit.*, p. 136.
49. DPL 7/6/2, *op. cit.*, meetings of 5 May and 11 June 1837.
50. *Renfrewshire Sasines*, 23 May 1837, No. 3909.
51. Donald Macleod, *The God's Acre of Dumbarton, op. cit.*, p. 231.
52. DPL 7/6/2, *op. cit.*, meeting of 4 November 1839.
53. *Ibid.*, meeting of 6 September 1839.
54. Information kindly supplied by Graham E Langmuir.
55. Donald Macleod, *The God's Acre of Dumbarton, op. cit.*, p. 231.
56. *Ibid.*
57. DPL 7/6/3, minute book of the Dumbarton Steamboat Companies No. 2, meeting of 12 December 1844.
58. Donald MacLeod, *The God's Acre of Dumbarton, op. cit.*, p. 231.
59. DPL 7/6/3, *op. cit.*, meeting of 26 November 1846, and, contract of co-partnery of 4 January 1847.
60. DPL 7/6/4, minute book of the Loch Lomond Steamboat Companies, pp. 20–74.
61. DPL 7/6/3, *op. cit.*, annual report, 1849.
62. Donald Macleod, *The God's Acre of Dumbarton, op. cit.*, p. 231.
63. SRO, SC65/34/6, inventory of the estate of James Lang, 15 June 1850.

Chapter 4
References

1. SRO, CS318/22/313, sequestration papers of McFadyen & Co, 1879.
2. GUA, GD320/4/1/1, balance sheet, etc., of Russell & Co, 1877.
3. Deduced from the surviving records and sequestration papers of the Greenock and Port Glasgow shipbuilders.
4. *Renfrewshire Sasines*, 17 March 1876, No. 405, and, 11 September 1878, No. 6641.
5. Ledger, P MacCallum & Sons Ltd in account with Pascoe Grenfell & Sons, 1876–1908 (PM & S).
6. SRO, CS318/26/1883/393, sequestration papers of James E Scott, 1879–83.
7. See S G Checkland, *Scottish Banking. A History, 1695–1973* (1975), pp. 469–77.
8. SRO, CS242/238, Petition of John Bell and others (James Lang of Dumbarton) for ratification of register of shareholders of the City of Glasgow Bank, 5 November 1878.
9. *Renfrewshire Sasines*, 11 October 1878, No. 6642, and, 28 October 1878, No. 6914.
10. GUA, extracts from the diaries and papers of Joseph Russell, 1834–1917, p. 15.
11. P L Payne, *Colvilles and the Scottish Steel Industry* (1979), pp. 45–55.
12. *Ibid.*, pp. 55–58, and, John R Hume and Michael S Moss, *Beardmore - The History of a Scottish Industrial Giant* (1979), pp. 32–3.
13. D L Burn, *The Economic History of Steel Making* (1940), pp. 156–8.
14. P L Payne, *op. cit.*, p. 57.
15. M S Moss, *William Todd Lithgow - Founder of a Fortune*, to be published in Scottish Historical Review, 1983.
16. GUA, GD320/4/2/1, Russell & Co, private ledger, 1890–99.
17. GUA, GD319/7/2/9, ledgers, Scotts Shipbuilding & Engineering Co.
18. Contract book No. 1, 1896–1902 (PM & S).
19. *Ibid.*
20. *Ibid.*
21. P L Payne, *op. cit.*, p. 105.
22. Contract book No. 1, 1896–1902 (PM & S).

24. *Ibid.*
25. Contract book No. 1, 1896-1902 (PM & S).
26. SRO, RDS 3320, trust disposition and settlement of John Lang, 3 November 1903, and, SRO, SC 65/34/18 inventory of John Lang, 1903.
27. GUA, Russell diaries, *op. cit.*, pp. 31-2.
28. Sketch of the life of John Lang contained in the Lang family bible.
29. *Ibid.*
30. Private ledger, *op. cit.*
31. Contract book No. 2, 1902-7 (PM S).
32. *Ibid.*
33. Private ledger, *op. cit.*
34. Share register of P MacCallum & Sons Ltd, 1907-28 (PM & S).
35. Information kindly supplied by Peter Lang.
36. Contract book No. 3, 1907-11 (PM & S).
37. Mark D Dykes, *The Scottish Iron Merchant of One Hundred Years Ago - Barclay & Mathieson Ltd* (1980), pp. 10-12.
38. Contract book No. 3, 1907-11 (PM & S).
39. Correspondence between Col. Wright and P MacCallum & Sons Ltd, 1908-11 (PM & S).
40. Lease in possession of PM & S.
41. Contract book No. 3, 1907-11 (PM & S).
42. London ledger No. 1, 1909-20.
43. Information kindly supplied by Peter Lang, and, share register, *op. cit.*
44. Contract book No. 3, 1907-11 (PM & S).
45. *Merchant Shipbuilding Under Government Control from May 1917 up to the Cessation of Hostilities* (1919), *passim.*
46. P L Payne, *op. cit.*, pp. 139-50, and, Hume and Moss, *op. cit.*, pp. 171-2.
47. F H Hatch, *The Iron and Steel Industry of the United Kingdom under War Conditions* (1919), *passim.*
48. Michael S Moss and John R Hume, *Workshop of the British Empire* (1977), pp. 104-5.
49. Correspondence between Russell & Co and Peter MacCallum & Sons Ltd (PM & S).
50. Minute book of P MacCallum & Sons Ltd. No. 1, 1908-30, meeting of 20 November 1919 (PM & S).

Chapter 5
References

1. Anne and Russell Long, *A Shipping Venture - Turnbull Scott and Company 1872-1972* (1974), pp. 57-82.
2. See, for example, J Cormack, 'Depreciation of Ships in relation to Income Tax', *Accountants Magazine* (1897), pp. 620-31.
3. *Century of Growth - An Historical Outline of the Denholm Group of Companies* (1972), pp. 8-10.
4. Greenock Statutory Register of Shipping, 1876-1877.
5. SRO, SC65/34/6, inventory of the estate of James Lang, 15 June 1850.
6. GUA, UGD95/3, Glasgow Underwriters' Admission Committee Minute Book, 1859-1914, p. 148.
7. *Short history of the Association of Underwriters and Insurance Brokers in Glasgow*, available from the Association.
8. C Watford, *Insurance Cyclopaedia (1872-78).*
9. Strathclyde Regional Archives, TD103/2/2 claims book No. 2 of the Association of Underwirters and Insurance in Glasgow.
10. Information kindly supplied by M Thomson, partner in Wigham & Poland, insurance brokers,
11. Greenock Statutory Register of Shipping, 1880.
12. Basil Greenhill, *The Ship. The Life and Death of the Merchant Sailing Ship* (1980), p. 28.
13. John Orbell, *From Cape to Cape - The History of Lyle Shipping* (1978), pp. 17-33.
14. Basil Greenhill, *op. cit.*, pp. 38-9.
15. PRO, BT/99/1613/62409, crew list of *Mary Low*, 1890.

16. PRO, BT/99/1613/62409, crew list of *Mary Low*, 1890.
17. GUA, GD320/5/3/5, cash book No. 5 of Robert Duncan & Co, ship Nos. 262–324.
18. Michael S Moss, *William Todd Lithgow - Founder of a Fortune*, to be published in Scottish Historical Review, 1983, pp. 4–5, and 25.
19. See, for example, John Orbell, *op. cit.*, pp. 54–68.
20. Minute book of the Ship East African Co (MBSEA) (PM & S).
21. SRO, BT2/2684, company file of the Ship East Indian Co, 1894–1909.
22. Midland Bank Archives, North and South Wales Bank board minutes, refs M22–M24.
23. MBSEA, annual report, 1896.
24. Michael S Moss, *op. cit.*, Table 4, capital structure of Russell & Co, 1892–1908.
25. GUA GD320/8/1/402, agreement, specification, correspondence, etc., relating to the *Australian*, Russell & Co, 1896.
26. *Ibid.*
27. Minute book of the Ship Australian Co (MBSA), 1896–1910 (PM & S).
28. SRO, BT2/2187, company file Dechmont Ship Co, 1891–1911.
29. Minute book Eastern Shipping Co (MBES), 1899–1911 (PM & S).
30. MBSA, annual reports, 1896–1900.
31. MBSEA, annual report, 1899.
32. MBSEA, MBSA, MBES, annual reports, 1900–1.
33. Information kindly supplied by Patricia Lang.
34. SRO, BT2/4575, company file Ship Edenmore Co, 1900–10.
35. Basil Greenhill, *op. cit.*, pp. 44–48, and, John Orbell, *op. cit.*, pp. 60–1.
36. MBES, annual report, 1904.
37. MBSEA, annual report, 1905.
38. MBSA, annual report, 1905.
39. *Ibid.*, and, MBSEA, annual report, 1905.
40. *Ibid.*
41. GUA, GD320/8/1/375, agreements, specifications, correspondence, etc. relating to the *Ormsary*, Russell & Co, 1902.
42. Information kindly supplied by Patricia Lang.
43. SRO, BT2/5236, company file Ship Ormsary Co, 1902–7.
44. Information kindly supplied by Patricia Lang.
45. *Ibid.*
46. GUA, GD320/8/1/446, agreements, specifications, correspondence, etc. relating to Russell & Co, ship No. 550.
47. Letter book of Lang & Fulton (LBLF), 1905–19, letters to W T Lithgow, 1905 (PM & S).
48. *Ibid.*, letters to potential investors, 1908.
49. GUA, GD320/8/1/446, *op. cit.*
50. LBLF, James Fulton to Charles D Toosey, 29 October 1905, p. 52.
51. SRO, BT2/5296, company file for the Steamship Ardgowan Co, 1906–15.
52. LBLF, pp. 134–5.
53. LBLF, James Fulton junior to Captain Coath, 6 December 1905, pp. 172–5.
54. SRO, BT2/5236, *op. cit.*
55. Information kindly supplied by Patricia Lang.
56. LBLF, letters 14 May 1907 to shareholders, pp. 208–10.
57. SRO, BT2/2702, company file Annasona Ship Co, 1894–1908, BT2/2701, company file Zinita Ship Co, 1894–1910, and, BT2/2700, company file Calluna Ship Co, 1894–1910.
58. MBSEA, MBSA, and, MBES, annual reports, 1907.
59. See, for example, MBSA, annual report, 1907.
60. Minute book Lang & Fulton (MBLF), 1907–24 (PM & S).
61. MBSEA, annual report, 1909.
62. *Ibid.*
63. Michael Moss, *op. cit.*, pp. 27–8.
64. LBLF, John J Lang to Captain Jones, 13 May 1909, pp. 241–3.
65. *Ibid.*, Lang & Fulton to Russell & Co, 17 September 1908.
66. *Ibid.*, same to same, 8 March 1909, MBLF, annual report, 1909.
67. Minute book Steamship Ardgryfe Co (MBS Ardgryfe), 1909–19.
68. See, for example, John Orbell, *op. cit.*, p. 64.

69. LBLF, John J Lang to Captain Jones, 13 May 1909, pp. 241-3.
70. Ship list, and, Basil Greenhill, *op. cit.*, p. 48.
71. MBSEA, annual reports, 1890-1910.
72. Basil Greenhill, *op. cit.*, p. 145, and, John Orbell, *op. cit.*, pp. 51-3.
73. PRO, BT165/275/102395, ship's log of *East African*, 1907.
74. Minute book Steamship Ardgoil Co (MBS Ardgoil), 1904-14 (PM & S), annual report, 1910.
75. MBS Ardgryfe, annual reports, 1909-11.
76. LBLF, J Fulton junior to William Hamilton & Co, 3 June 1910 and MBLF, annual report, 1910.
77. LBLF, J Fulton junior to Henry Lithgow, 14 November 1911, and, minute book of Steamship Ardgarroch Co (MBS Ardgarroch), 1911-19 (PM & S).
78. MBS Ardgoil, Ardgryfe, and Ardgarroch, annual reports, 1911.
79. LBLF, J Fulton junior to Robert Duncan & Co, 15 December 1911, pp. 372-4, and, GUA, GD320/5/5, cash book No. 5 of Robert Duncan & Co, ship Nos. 262-324.
80. Minute book Ard Coasters Ltd (MBAC), 1903-22 (PM & S).
81. Minute book, Steamship Ardgair Co (MBS Ardgair), 1913-14, list of subscribers 1913 (PM & S).
82. D H Aldcroft, 'The Depression in British Shipping 1901-1911', *Journal of Transport History*, VII (1965), p. 19.
83. LBLF, J Fulton junior to F Todd, 5 April 1913, p. 320.
84. MBS Ardgoil, annual report, 1913.
85. Minute book, Steamship Ardgarry (MBS Ardgarry), 1914-21, (PM & S).
86. Strathclyde Regional Archives, TD103/1/3, minute book No. 2 of the Association of Insurance Brokers and Underwriters in Glasgow, p. 328.
87. GUA, GD95/3, *op. cit.*, pp. 308 and 326.
88. *Ibid.*, p. 338.
89. John Orbell, *op. cit.*, p. 65.
90. S G Sturmey, *British Shipping and World Competition* (1962), p. 49.
91. MBS Ardgarry, annual report, 1915.
92. MBS Ardgair, annual reports, 1915 and 1916.
93. MBS Ardgorm, annual reports, 1915 and 1916.
94. MBLF, annual reports, 1914-16.
95. *Ibid.*
96. *Ibid.*
97. *Ibid.*
98. *Ibid.*
99. J M Reid, *James Lithgow - Master of Work* (1964), pp. 45-58.
100. GUA, GD320/1/1/526, agreements, specifications, correspondence, etc. *Ardgrange* and *Ardgask*, Russell & Co, 1915.
101. MBLF, annual report, 1915.
102. *Ibid.*, annual report, 1917.
103. *Ibid.*
104. Minute book Ard Steamers Ltd (MBAS), 1917-22, (PM & S), list of subscribers.
105. MBLF, annual report, 1917.
106. MBS Ardgorm, annual report, 1917.
107. *Merchant Shipbuilding Under Government Control from May 1917 up to the Cessation of Hostilities* (1919), *passim*.
108. MBS Ardgarry, and, MBAS, annual reports, 1918.
109. MBAS, annual report, 1918.
110. Ship list.
111. *Ibid.*
112. *The Times*, 11 November 1926, p. 21.
113. Edwin Green and Michael Moss, *A Company of National Importance - A History of the Kylsant Group of Companies*, to be published 1982, chapter 5.
114. J M Reid, *op. cit.*, pp. 45-70.

General note: details of changes in the membership of the Board and of share transfers are drawn from the Minute Books of P MacCallum & Sons Ltd (PM & SMB)

1. S G Sturmey, *British Shipping and World Competition*, pp. 56–9.
2. D L Burn, *The Economic History of Steelmaking 1867–1939*, Cambridge, 1940, pp. 350–6.
3. PM & S, Abstract Contract Book, 1911–33.
4. PM & SMB No. 1, meeting of 20 November 1919.
5. GUA GD320/4/1/45, Lithgows Ltd, Balance Sheets, Profit and Loss Accounts; P L Payne, *Colvilles and the Scottish Steel Industry*, Oxford, 1979, p. 148.
6. GUA, GD320/4/1/45.
7. PM & S, Balance Sheet, 1919.
8. P L Payne, *Colvilles*, p. 148.
9. *Ibid.*, pp. 139–47; also J R Hume and M S Moss, *Beardmore: The History of a Scottish Industrial Giant*, 1979, pp. 171–2.
10. GUA, GD320/2/4, joint account book of Henry and James Lithgow, 1919–21.
11. *Stock Exchange Yearbook*, 1920.
12. PM & S, miscellaneous correspondence.
13. PM & SMB No. 1, meeting of 1 July 1920.
14. *Ibid.*, meeting of 20 December 1920.
15. PM & S, miscellaneous correspondence.
16. PM & SMB vol 1, meeting of 29 December 1920.
17. Payne, *Colvilles*, p. 148.
18. PM & S, Balance Sheet, 1921.
19. *Ibid.*
20. Burn, *Steelmaking*, pp. 393, 402–4.
21. PM & S, Abstract Contract Book, 1911–33.
22. *Ibid.*
23. PM & S, Balance Sheet, 1922.
24. PM & S, Abstract Contract Book, 1911–33.
25. PM & S, Balance Sheet, 1923.
26. PM & SMB No. 1, meeting of 25 October 1923.
27. *Ibid.*, meeting of 24 October 1923.
28. *Ibid.*
29. PM & S, Abstract Contract Book, 1911–33.
30. *Ibid.* The rest of this paragraph is based on the same source.
31. PM & SMB No. 1, meeting of 4 April 1924.
32. Information supplied by the Lang family.
33. PM & SMB No. 1, meeting of 12 September 1924.
34. *Greenock Telegraph*.
35. Information from I B Lang and from Wigham Poland Scotland Ltd.
36. PM & S, Abstract Contract Book, 1911–33.
37. PM & S, Balance Sheet, 1925.
38. *Shipbuilding & Shipping Record*, Vol. 25, 1925, p. 49.
39. PM & SMB No. 1, meeting of 2 July 1925.
40. *Ibid.*, meetings of 27 May and 17 December 1925.
41. Payne, *Colvilles*, p. 149.
42. PM & S, Abstract Contract Book, 1911–33.
43. PM & S, Balance Sheet, 1925.
44. PM & S, Abstract Contract Book, 1911–33, pencil notes.
45. *Shipbuilding & Shipping Record*, Vol. 27, 1926, p. 682; *Register of Defunct Companies*.
46. J P Addis, 'The Heavy Iron & Steel Industry in South Wales 1870–1950', Unpublished PhD thesis, University of Wales, 1957.
47. *Shipbuilding & Shipping Record*, Vol. 28, 1926, p. 639.
48. PM & SMB No. 1, meeting of 28 December 1925.
49. *Ibid.*, meeting of 15 April 1926.

50. PM & S, Abstract Contract Book, 1911–33.
51. PM & S, Balance Sheet, 1927.
52. PM & SMB No. 1, meeting of 10 February 1927; *Lloyds Register*.
53. PM & S, miscellaneous correspondence, and typescript, Mark D Dykes, 'The Scottish Iron Merchant of 100 years ago, a Centenary History of Barclay & Matheson Ltd'.
54. PM & S File, NFISM.
55. PM & S File: Reduction of Capital, 1928, PM & SMB No. 1, meetings of 13 and 31 January, 16 February, 11 April, 31 May and 7 June 1928.
56. *Ibid.*, meeting of 21 June 1928.
57. *Ibid.*, meetings of 10 and 25 October 1928.
58. PM & S, Abstract Contract Book, 1911–13.
59. PM & S, Balance Sheet, 1928.
60. PM & SMB No. 1, meeting of 31 May 1928.
61. PM & S, Abstract Contract Book, 1911–33; Payne, *Colvilles*, p. 149.
62. PM & S, Balance Sheet, 1929.
63. *Greenock Telegraph*, 17 June 1929.
64. Information from the Lang family.
65. *Glasgow Herald*, 28 April 1930; see also *Greenock Telegraph* of the same date.
66. PM & S, Abstract Contract Book, 1911–33.
67. Payne, *Colvilles*, p. 169; see also Burn, *Steelmaking*, pp. 438–40.
68. Harland & Wolff Ltd, Minute Book D, meeting of 3 June 1930.
69. E Green and M Moss, *A Business of National Importance: The Royal Mail Shipping Group, 1902–37*, Methuen, London, 1982.
70. Hume and Moss, *Beardmore*, pp. 238–9. Most of the rest of this paragraph is based on Payne, *Colvilles*, pp. 180–210.
71. PM & S, Abstract Contract Books, 1911–33 and 1934–65.
72. Burn, *Steelmaking*, p. 451.
73. *Ibid.*, p. 439.
74. PM & S File, NFISM.
75. PM & S, Abstract Contract Books, 1911–33 and 1934–65.
76. See for example Hume and Moss, *Beardmore*, p. 197.
77. Green and Moss, *Royal Mail*, p. 90.
78. *Ibid.*, p. 215.
79. *Ibid.*
80. National Shipbuilders Security Minute Book, January 1936.
81. Payne, *Colvilles*, p. 183.
82. PM & S, Abstract Contract Book, 1911–33.
83. PM & S, Balance Sheets, 1931–3.
84. PM & SMB No. 2, meeting of 23 December 1932.
85. PM & SMB No. 2, meeting of 19 December 1933.
86. Burn, *Steelmaking*, pp. 449–55.
87. *Ibid.*, pp. 381–2 and 453–5.
88. PM & S, Abstract Contract Book, 1934–65. The rest of this paragraph and the whole of the next are based on this source.
89. PM & SMB No. 2, meetings of 8 and 15 March 1935.
90. *Ibid.*, meeting of 15 May 1936.
91. *Ibid.*, meeting of 18 August 1936.
92. *Ibid.*, meeting of 22 December 1937.
93. Abstract Log Book (PM & S Ships), folios 57–62.
94. PM & SMB No. 2, meeting of 22 December 1938.
95. PM & S, Balance Sheets 1934–7.
96. *Greenock Telegraph*, 17 May 1934.
97. Information from Wigham Poland Scotland Ltd and I B Lang.
98. *Greenock Telegraph*.
99. PM & SMB No. 2, meeting of 22 December 1937.
100. Information from Lang family.

101. M M Postan, *British War Production*, HMSO 1952, p. 91; W K Hancock and M M Gowing, *The British War Economy*, HMSO 1949, p. 23 and Chapter 4, section 3.
102. PM & SMB No. 2, meeting of 29 December 1939.
103. *Ibid.*, meetings of 24 August and 11 September 1939.
104. PM & SMB No. 2, meetings of 29 December 1939; 26 February 1942, 26 February 1943, 17 February 1944.
105. PM & S, Abstract Log Book (MV *Ardglass, Ardgarvel*).
106. PM & SMB No. 2, meetings of 30 December 1940, 18 February 1941; see also Abstract Log Book (PM & S ships), folios 74-6, 79-85.
107. PM & S, Balance Sheet, 1940.
108. PM & SMB No. 2, meeting of 26 February 1942.
109. PM & S, Abstract Log Book (PM & S ships), folios 67-70.
110. PM & SMB No. 2, meeting of 26 February 1942; see also Abstract Log Book (PM & S ships), folios 86-8; *Lloyd's Register*.
111. PM & S, Balance Sheet, 1941.
112. *Lloyd's Register*.
113. PM & S, Balance Sheets, 1943, 1944.
114. PM & SMB No. 2, meeting of 28 December 1944.
115. *Ibid.*, meetings of 18 February 1941, 25 December 1941 and 26 February 1942.
116. *Ibid.*, meeting of 26 February 1942.
117. *Ibid.*, meetings of 17 February 1944, 28 December 1944.
118. *Ibid.*
119. Details of the war service of members of the Lang and Fulton families have been supplied by their relatives.
120. The Minute Book of the Kindiesel Shipping Co Ltd is the source for most of this section.
121. Abstract Log Book (MV *Ardglen, Ardgantock*).
122. *Yachting*, February 1941, August 1941.

Chapter 7
References

General note: details of changes in the membership of the Board and of share transfers are drawn from the Minute Books of Peter MacCallum & Sons Ltd (PM & SMB)
1. B S Keeling and A E G Wright, *The Development of the Modern British Steel Industries*, London, 1964, pp. 99-100.
2. PM & S File, NFISS.
3. PM & SMB No. 2, meeting of 27 December 1945.
4. *Ibid.*, meeting of 27 December 1946.
5. *Ibid.*, meeting of 25 February 1949.
6. *Ibid.*, meeting of 12 March 1951, PM & SMB No. 3, meeting of 21 March 1952.
7. *Ibid.*, meeting of 27 December 1945.
8. PM & S, Accounts, 1945, 1946.
9. PM & SMB No. 2, meeting of 9 March 1950.
10. PM & S, Accounts, 1945, 1946.
11. *Ibid.*, 1946-50; PM & SMB No. 2, meeting of 9 March 1950.
12. *Ibid.*, meeting of 30 June 1950.
13. PM & S, Accounts, 1950.
14. PM & SMB No. 3, meeting of 14 April 1951.
15. PM & S Abstract Voyage Book (MV *Ardglen, Ardgantock*).
16. PM & S, Accounts, 1950, 1951.
17. Keeling and Wright, *The Development of the Modern British Steel Industries*, pp. 164-72.
18. PM & S, File 'Annual Tonnages'.
19. PM & S, Accounts, 1953.
20. PM & S, Abstract Log Book (MV *Ardglen, Ardgantock*).
21. *Greenock Telegraph*, 9 February 1957 and notes in PM & S Scrap Book.
22. Information supplied by Mrs McLaren, Abstract Log Book (MV *Ardglen, Ardgantock*).

23. PM & SMB No. 3, meeting of 2 April 1955.
24. *Ibid.*, meeting of 24 October 1955.
25. PM & S, Abstract Log Book (MV *Ardglen, Ardgantock*).
26. PM & S, Accounts, 1957-9.
27. PM & SMB No. 3, meeting of 2 December 1959; *Lloyd's Register*.
28. *Ibid.*, meeting of 30 June 1954.
29. PM & S, Abstract Contract Book, 1934-65.
30. See for instance M S Moss and J R Hume, *Workshop of the British Empire*, 1977, pp. 110-12, 141-4.
31. PM & S, Abstract Contract Book, 1934-65.
32. *Ibid.*
33. Information from the Lang family.
34. Information from John Macdonald, Director PM & S.
35. *Ibid.*
36. Letter from George Currie & Sons.
37. Information from John Macdonald.
38. PM & SMB No. 2, meeting of 27 December 1945.
39. *Ibid.*, meeting of 30 December 1947.
40. PM & SMB No. 3, meetings of 21 March 1952, 6 February 1953.
41. *Ibid.*, meeting of 25 February 1956.
42. PM & S, Accounts, 1958-61.
43. PM & S, Accounts, 1965.
44. Information from P M Lang.
45. PM & S, File 'Scrap Business'; PM & SMB No. 3, meeting of 10 January 1968; information from Peter Lang.
46. PM & S, Abstract Contract Book, 1934-65.
47. PM & S, File Shipping Department Reports.
48. PM & SMB No. 3, meeting of 22 February 1963; *Lloyd's List*, 3 October 1963.
49. *Daily Mail*, 8 October 1963.
50. PM & SMB No. 3, 15 October 1963.
51. PM & S, Abstract Log Book (MV *Ardglen, Ardgantock*).
52. *Glasgow Herald*, 30 November 1968, 18 March 1969.
53. *Glasgow Herald*, 3 March 1972.
54. PM & S, Accounts, 1962-9.
55. PM & S, File T D R Taylor.
56. *Glasgow Herald*, 13 March 1961.
57. Information from John Macdonald.
58. PM & S, File SDA, 1967-72.
59. PM & S, File SDA, 1967-72; information from R L V Fulton.
12. Obituary in *Greenock Telegraph*, November 1981.
61. *Ibid.*, meeting of 15 August 1974.
62. PM & S, File Shipping Department Reports.
63. PM & SMB No. 3, meeting of 15 August 1974.
64. *Ibid.*, meeting of 25 November 1974; *Lloyd's Register*.
65. PM & SMB No. 3, meeting of 17 April 1974.

Chapter 8
References

1. John Orbell, *From Cape to Cape: the History of Lyle Shipping*, Edinburgh, 1978, pp. 163-72.
2. PM & SMB No. 3, meeting of 1 April 1975.
3. *Ibid.*, meeting of 14 September 1976.
4. *Ibid.*, meeting of 1 April 1975.
5. Information supplied by Mr W Cochrane, Director of Cochranes (Bo'ness) Ltd; *Slater's Directories of Scotland, passim.*
6. SRO BT2/8267.

7. Registered Companies Office SC 17099.
8. Information from R L V Fulton.
9. Information from the Lang family.
10. *Ibid.*, see also *Greenock Telegraph*, 23 March 1981.
11. Information from P M Lang.
12. Obituary in *Greenock Telegraph*, November 1981.

Ship List

Ship List
Part One
The Sailing Fleet of Lang & Fulton 1876–1912

1. *Lady Clarendon* (1876–81)
   1,296 net tons
   1853 completed at New Brunswick, 1876 acquired by John and William Low, shipowners, Greenock, and James Fulton and John Lang, iron merchants, Greenock.

2. *Eirene* (1877–*c.* 1882)
   1877 purchased by William Rankin, shipowner, Greenock, and John Lang, iron merchant, Greenock. *c.* 1882 sold to Thomas H Gibbs of London.

3. *Alexandra* (1880–3)
   Fully rigged ship.
   1,400 gross tons, 915 net tons
   164 × 36 × 22 feet
   1863 completed by Messrs Raymond, Pleasant Cove, Nova Scotia, for Shaw & Co., Yarmouth, Nova Scotia. 1870s sold to A C Robbins, Yarmouth, Nova Scotia. 1880 purchased by Lang & Fulton and converted to a barque. 1883 wrecked.

4. *East Anglian* (1886–96)
   Iron Barque
   1,900 gross tons, 912 net tons
   197 × 32 × 19 feet
   1876 completed by Robert Duncan & Co, cost of £13,450, for John Low of Greenock as *Mary Low*. 1866 purchased by Lang & Fulton, renamed *East Anglian* and placed in the ownership of The Ship East Anglia Co. 1896 stranded Penarth head on passage Cardiff to Esquimalt. Abandoned to underwriters, refloated, repaired, and sold to Chr Hieizen, Larwig, Norway.

5. *East Indian* (1894–1910)
   Steel barque, fitted with top and gallant yards
   1,745 gross tons, 1,603 net tons
   252 × 19 × 22 feet
   May 1894 completed by Robert Duncan & Co, Port Glasgow, cost of £13,500 for The Ship East Indian Co. 1910 sold to G Krabbenhoft, Hamburg, and renamed *Hans*.

6. *East African* (1895–1911)
   Steel barque
   2,850 gross tons, 1,731 net tons
   252 × 39 × 22 feet
   Feb. 1895 completed by Robert Duncan & Co, Port Glasgow, cost of £13,000 for The Ship East African Co. 1911 sold to A T Simonsen, Christiania.

7. *Deccan* (1897)
   Steel ship fitted with double fore main top gallant and royals
   3,000 gross tons, 985 net tons
   266 × 40 × 23 feet
   March 1897 completed by Robert Duncan & Co, Port Glasgow, cost of £15,092, for Lang & Fulton, sold immediately to British & Eastern Shipping Co.

8. *Australian* (1897–1908)
   Steel ship fitted with double fore main top gallant and royals
   3,450 gross tons 2,103 net tons
   270 × 40 × 23 feet
   Jan. 1897 completed by Russell & Co, Port Glasgow, cost of £15,000 for The Ship Australian Co. 1908 lost with all hands on passage from Mugattan to Sydney.

9. *Dechmont* (1898–1918)
   Steel ship
   1,727 gross tons, 1,642 net tons
   260 × 38 × 23 feet
   July 1891 completed by Russell & Co, at a cost of £17,410 for The Dechmont Ship Co (managers A R Thom & Co), Glasgow. 1898 The Dechmont Ship Co acquired by Lang & Fulton. 1910 sold to H E Hansen, Lillesand, Norway.

10. *Grenada* (1899–1910)
    Steel four masted barque
    2,268 gross tons, 2,106 net tons
    278 × 42 × 24 feet
    Nov. 1894 completed by Russell & Co at a cost of £18,000 for P Denniston & Co, Glasgow. 1899 half share purchased by Lang & Fulton Ltd and placed in the ownership of the Eastern Shipping Co. 1910 sold to Geralia Ship Co.

11. *Edenmore* (1901–9)
    Steel ship
    1,726 gross tons, 1,642 net tons
    260 × 38 × 23 feet
    March 1890 completed by Russell & Co as *Edenballymore*, at a cost of £18,300 for Sailing Ship Edenballymore Co (managers Thomson, Dickie & Co), Glasgow. 1901 purchased by Lang & Fulton, renamed *Edenmore*, and placed in the ownership of The Ship Edenmore Co. 1909 blown ashore at Papa Stronsay, Orkney on passage from Hamburg for Sydney and became a total loss.

12. *Ormsary* (1903–6)
    Steel four masted barque
    2,251 gross tons
    Jan. 1903 completed by Russell & Co (the last sailing vessel built by the firm) for The Ship Ormsary Co. 1906 lost with all hands off Cape Horn.

13. *Kynance* (1903–10)
    Steel ship
    3,250 gross tons, 1,964 net tons
    265 × 36 × 22 feet
    Nov. 1895 completed by Anderson Rodger & Co, Port Glasgow, for The Sailing Ship Kynance Co (managers C G Cowan & Co), Greenock. 1903 The Sailing Ship Kynance Co acquired by Lang & Fulton. 1910 stranded at Puerta Blanca, off Tocopilla, in calm, on passage from Valparaiso and became a total loss.

Part Two
Sailing ships managed by Lang & Fulton 1900–10

1. *Arana*
   Steel ship
   1911 completed for A Mackay & Co, Glasgow 1895 sold to J D Clink, Greenock. 1900 placed under management of Lang & Fulton and lost with all hands on passage from Santa Rosalia.

2. *Valkyrie* (1900)
   Steel ship
   2,270 gross tons
   283 × 42 × 24 feet
   1892 completed by Charles Connell & Co, Glasgow, for Valkyrie Ship Co (managers J D Clink) Greenock. 1900 placed under management of Lang & Fulton and wrecked in the River Elbe.

3. *Thistle* (1904–5)
   Steel four-masted barque
   2,289 gross tons
   284 × 42 × 24 feet
   1891 completed by Charles Connell & Co, Glasgow, for Thistle Ship Co (managers J D Clink) Greenock. 1904 placed under management of Lang & Fulton. 1905 wrecked on Palmerston Island, Port Pirrie, Portland, Oregon.

4. *Ancona* (1906)
   Steel ship
   2,852 gross tons
   280 × 44 × 22 feet
   Nov. 1893 completed by Russell & Co, Port Glasgow, for The Ship Ancona Co (managers G T Soley & Co), Liverpool. 1906 placed under the management of Lang & Fulton and burnt out in the Bay of Biscay.

5. *Amasana* (1907)
Steel barque
2,900 gross tons, 1,436 net tons
239 × 36 × 21 feet
1892 completed by Charles Connell & Co, Glasgow, for Amasana Ship Co (managers J D Clink), Greenock. 1907 placed under the management of Lang & Fulton and wrecked in Australia.

6. *Samoena* (1907–10)
Steel ship
3,300 gross tons, 1,962 net tons
272 × 40 × 23 feet
1892 completed by Charles Connell & Co, Glasgow, for Samoena Ship Co (managers J D Clink) Greenock. 1907 placed under the management of Lang & Fulton. 1910 sold to J A Zachariorssen, Nystad, Finland.

7. *Calluna* (1907–10)
Steel barque
2,300 gross tons, 1,346 net tons
230 × 36 × 21 feet
1891 completed by Charles Connell & Co, Glasgow, for Calluna Ship Co (managers J D Clink) Greenock. 1907 placed under the management of Lang & Fulton. 1910 sold to R Harsen, Christiania, Norway.

8. *Zinita*
Steel barque
2,750 gross tons, 1,633 net tons
260 × 38 × 21 feet
1893 completed by Charles Connell & Co, Glasgow, for Zinita Ship Co (managers J D Clink), Greenock. 1967 placed under the management of Lang & Fulton. 1910 sold to J Brun, Tønsberg, Norway.

Part Three
The Ard Steamship Fleet of Lang & Fulton 1906–22

1. *Ardgowan* (1906–15)
7,300 gross tons, 4,271 net tons
369 × 49 × 19 feet
Triple expansion 3 cylinder engines built by Rankin & Blackmore Ltd, Greenock
Jan. 1906 completed by Russell & Co, Port Glasgow for The Steamship Ardgowan Co, cost £42,000. 1915 sold to Westminster Shipping Co for £66,000, renamed *Mesopotamia*.

2. *Ardgoil* (1909–13)
7,600 gross tons, 4,395 net tons
385 × 49 × 18 feet
Triple expansion 3 cylinder engines built by Clyde Shipbuilding & Engineering Co, Port Glasgow
July 1909 completed by Russell & Co, Port Glasgow for The Steamship Ardgoil Co, cost £40,000. 1913 sold to W Thomas Sons & Co, Liverpool for £46,000, renamed *Globe*.

3. *Ardgryfe* (1909–18)
8,500 gross tons, 4,897 net tons
400 × 52 × 27 feet
Triple expansion 3 cylinder engines built by Rankin & Blackmore Ltd, Greenock
Sept. 1909 completed by Russell & Co, for The Steamship Ardgryfe Co, cost £43,000. 1918 sold to Cayzer Irvine & Co's Clan Line, renamed *Clan Kenneth*.

4. *Santa Rosalia* (1911)
9,500 gross tons, 5,409 net tons
406 × 52 × 23 feet
Triple expansion 3 cylinder engines built by John G Kincaid & Co, Greenock
Sept. 1911 completed by William Hamilton & Co, on joint account with Lang & Fulton Ltd, sold before delivery to Isthian Steamship Co.

5. *Ardgarroch* (1911–18)
   8,500 gross tons, 4,936 net tons
   400 × 52 × 19 feet
   Triple expansion 3 cylinder engines built by Rankin & Blackmore Ltd, Greenock
   Jan. 1907, completed by Russell & Co at a cost of £44,000 for Robertson, Shackland & Co (Burn Line), Greenock, owned by Withburn Steamship Co. 1911 purchased for £41,000 by Lang & Fulton for the Steamship Ardgarroch Co. 1918 sold to Cayzer Irvine & Co's Clan Line, renamed *Clan Kennedy*.

6. *Ardgair* (1913–18)
   8,500 gross tons, 5,000 net tons
   406 × 53 × 27 feet
   Triple expansion 3 cylinder engines built by John G Kincaid, Greenock
   May 1913, completed by Robert Duncan & Co, Port Glasgow, cost £50,000, for the Steamship Ardgair Co. 1918 sold to Furness Withy & Co's Prince Line, renamed *Manchurian Prince*.

7. *Ardgarth* (1913–24)
   1,050 gross tons, 770 net tons
   200 × 29 × 13 feet
   Triple expansion cylinder engines built by Ross & Duncan, Glasgow. Sept 1913, completed by George Brown & Co, Greenock, for Ard Coasters Ltd. 1922 transferred to P MacCallum & Sons Ltd. 1924 sold to Northminster Steamship Co (Richards, Longstaff & Co, managers) London renamed *Yorkminster*.

8. *Ardgorm* (1913–17)
   8,500 gross tons, 5,131 net tons
   405 × 53 × 27 feet
   Triple expansion 3 cylinder engines built by John G Kincaid, Greenock
   Dec. 1913, completed by Robert Duncan & Co, Port Glasgow, cost £60,000 for the Steamship Ardgorm Co. 1917 sold to Norfolk and North American Steam Shipping Co, for £175,000, transferred to Johnstone Line Ltd (managers Furness Withy) London, and renamed *Hartland Point*.

9. *Ardglass* (1914–17)
   1,050 gross tons, 778 net tons
   200 × 209 × 12 feet
   Triple expansion 3 cylinder engines built by Ross & Duncan, Glasgow
   Jan. 1914, completed by George Brown & Co, Greenock, for Ard Coasters Ltd. March 1917 captured by *U-65* in the Irish Sea and sunk with explosives, four miles east of Arklow light vessel.

10. *Ardgarry* (1913–19)
    7,900 gross tons, 4,526 net tons
    384 × 52 × 26 feet
    Triple expansion 3 cylinder engines built by Rankin & Blackmore, Greenock
    Dec. 1913, launched by Russell & Co, Port Glasgow, as *Loch-Na-Torran*, sold to Lang & Fulton and delivered to the Steamship Ardgarry Co. 1919 sold to Johnstone Line Ltd (managers Furness Withy) and renamed *Starhope*.

11. *Ardgour* (1914–22)
    1,050 gross tons, 778 net tons
    200 × 29 × 12 feet
    Triple expansion 3 cylinder engines by Rankin & Blackmore, Greenock
    March 1914, completed by George Brown & Co, Greenock, for Ard Coasters Ltd. 1922 transferred to P MacCallum & Sons Ltd. 1929 sold to Richards, Longstaff & Co, London, renamed *Yorkdale*.

12. *Ardgrange* (1916–19)
    7,900 gross tons, 4,543 net tons
    385 × 52 × 26 feet
    Triple expansion 3 cylinder engines built by Clyde Ship Building & Engineering Co, Port Glasgow
    Oct. 1916, completed by Russell & Co, Port Glasgow, at a cost of £73,000, for The Steamship Ardgrange Co. 1919 sold to Johnston Line Ltd (Furness Withy managers), London, and renamed *Nigmore*.

13. *Ardgask* (1916–18)
7,900 gross tons, 4,542 net tons
385 × 52 × 26 feet
Triple expansion 3 cylinder engines built by Clyde Ship Building & Engineering Co, Port Glasgow
Dec. 1916, completed by Russell & Co, Port Glasgow, cost £80,000 for the Steamship Ardgarry Co 1917 torpedoed and sunk by *U35*, 15 miles west of Cape Rosello, Sicily, with one life lost.

14. *Ardgarvel* (1917–22)
1,100 gross tons, 834 net tons
200 × 30 × 12 feet
Triple expansion 3 cylinder engines built by Ferguson Bros (Port Glasgow) Ltd, Port Glasgow
Jan. 1917, completed by Ferguson Bros (Port Glasgow) Ltd, Port Glasgow. 1922 transferred to P MacCallum & Sons Ltd. 1927 sold to Union Steamships Ltd, Vancouver, for £13,000 and renamed *Chillicrack*.

15. *Sycamore* (1917)
10,600 gross tons, 6,550 net tons
445 × 58 × 31 feet
Triple expansion 3 cylinder engines built by Rankin & Blackmore Ltd, Greenock
July 1917, completed by Robert Duncan & Co, Port Glasgow, for Lang & Fulton and sold to Johnston Line Ltd (managers Furness Withy Ltd), London.

16. *Ardglamis* (1917)
7,900 gross tons, 4,563 net tons
385 × 52 × 26 feet
Triple expansion 3 cylinder engines built by Clyde Ship Building & Engineering Co
Oct. 1917, completed by Russell & Co, Port Glasgow, cost £90,000 for the Steamship Ardgarry Co. Nov. 1917 torpedoed and sunk by *U-63*, 125 miles west of Cape Spartel on her maiden voyage with no loss of life.

17. *Ardgoil* (II) (1917–20)
8,800 gross tons, 5,318 net tons
405 × 52 × 27 feet
Triple expansion 3 cylinder engines built by John G Kincaid & Co, Greenock
Dec. 1917, completed by William Hamilton & Co, Port Glasgow, for Ard Steamers Ltd. 1920 sold to William Thomson & Co (Ben Line), Edinburgh and renamed *Bengloe*.

18. *Ardgay* (1917–19)
7,900 gross tons, 4,593 net tons
385 × 52 × 26 feet
Triple expansion 3 cylinder engines built by Rankin & Blackmore Ltd, Greenock
Dec. 1917, completed by Russell & Co, Port Glasgow, cost £90,000, for the Steamship Ardgarry Co. 1919 sold to Johnstone Line Ltd (Furness Withy & Co, managers), London, and renamed *Ernemore*.

19. *Ardgartock* (1917–18) 1,100 net tons 834 gross tons 200 × 30 × 12 feet. Triple expansion 3 cylinder engines built by Ferguson Bros (Port Glasgow) Ltd, Port Glasgow
Dec. 1917, completed by Ferguson Bros (Port Glasgow) Ltd, Port Glasgow. 1918 run down by HMS *Tartar*

20. *Ardglass* (II) (1918)
7,900 gross tons, 4,617 net tons
385 × 52 × 26 feet
Triple expansion 3 cylinder engines built by John G Kincaid & Co, Greenock
Jan. 1918, completed by Russell & Co, Port Glasgow, cost £87,500, for the Steamship Ardgarry Co. April 1918 torpedoed and sunk by *U-31* 6 miles east of the Maidens, with the loss of six lives, on her maiden voyage on Italian Government service.

21. *Ardgarry* (III) (1918–19)
7,900 gross tons, 4,580 net tons
385 × 52 × 26
Triple expansion 3 cylinder engines built by Rankin & Blackmore Ltd, Greenock
June 1918, completed by Russell & Co, Port Glasgow, cost of £87,500, for the Steamship Ardgarry Co. 1919 sold to Gulf Line Ltd (Furness Withy & Co, managers) and renamed *Comino*.

22. *Ardgowan* (II) (1918–22)
   8,500 gross tons, 5,334 net tons
   405 × 52 × 27 feet
   Triple expansion 3 cylinder engines built by J & G Kincaid Ltd
   July 1918, completed by William Hamilton & Co, for Ard Steamers Ltd. 1922 sold to G & J Thompson (Silver Line) London and renamed *Silverash*.
23. *Ardgartan* (1918–19)
   2,150 gross tons, 1,345 net tons
   229 × 35 × 15 feet
   Triple expansion 3 cylinder engine built by Ross & Duncan & Co, Glasgow
   1918 completed by Campbeltown Shipbuilding Co, Campbeltown, for the Steamship Ardgartan Co. 1919 lost with all hands on passage from Swansea to Brest with a cargo of coal.
24. *Ardgroom* (1918–19)
   7,900 gross tons, 4,882 net tons
   385 × 52 × 26 feet
   Triple expansion 3 cylinder engine built by Rankin & Blackmore Ltd, Greenock
   Aug. 1918, launched as *Ardgask II*, October 1918, completed as *Ardgroom* by Russell & Co, Port Glasgow, for the Steamship Ardgarry Co. 1919 sold to Johnson Line Ltd (managers Furness Withy), London, and renamed *Tullamore*.
25. *Ardgirvan* (1918–19)
   2,150 gross tons, 1,342 net tons
   230 × 35 × 15 feet
   Triple expansion 3 cylinder engine built by Ross & Duncan & Co, Glasgow
   Oct. 1918, completed by Campbeltown Shipbuilding Co, Campbeltown, for the Steamship Ardgartan Co. 1919 sold to European Gas Co (H A Brightman managers), London, and renamed *Bolvec*.
26. *Ardgryfe* (II) (1919)
   1,320 gross tons, 964 net tons
   200 × 31 × 13 feet
   Triple expansion 3 cylinder engine built by Aitchison Blair Ltd, Glasgow
   March 1918, completed by Ardrossan Dry Dock & Shipbuilding Co, Ardrossan, for Mead Son & Hussey, London, as *St Dunstan's Mill*. 1919 purchased by Lang & Fulton for P MacCallum & Son Ltd. 1922 sold to R MacCallum & Sons of Greenock for £39,053.
27. *Ardgarroch* (II) (1918–22)
   2,150 gross tons, 964 net tons
   200 × 31 × 13 feet
   Triple expansion 3 cylinder engine built by Aitchison Blair Ltd, Glasgow
   Dec. 1918, completed by Ardrossan Dry Dock and Shipbuilding Co, Ardrossan, for Mead Son & Hussey, London, as *Portland House*. 1919 purchased by Lang and Fulton for P MacCallum & Sons Ltd. 1937 sold to Bristol Steam Navigation Co, Bristol, and renamed *Capito*.
28. *Ardglass* (III) (1919)
   2,000 gross tons, 845 net tons
   200 × 30 × 12 feet
   Triple expansion engine built by Aitchison Blair Ltd, Glasgow
   Oct. 1919 completed by J Fullerton & Co, Paisley for P MacCallum & Sons Ltd. 1935 sold for £6,000 to Monroe Bros, Liverpool, and renamed *Kyle Castle*.
29. *Ardgantock* (II) (1919)
   2,000 gross tons, 845 net tons
   200 × 30 × 12 feet
   Triple expansion engine built by Aitchison Blair Ltd, Glasgow
   Laid down as *War Tummel*, June 1919. Completed by Ardrossan Dry Dock & Shipbuilding Co for P MacCallum & Sons Ltd. 1955 sold to Monroe Bros, Liverpool, and renamed *Kyle Castle*.

Part Four
Steamship Managed for the Shipping Controller by Lang & Fulton Ltd 1918–20

1. *War Fantail* (1918–20)
   7,800 gross tons, 4,453 net tons
   375 × 51 × 26 feet
   Triple expansion 3 cylinder engine built by Rankin & Blackmore Ltd, Greenock
   1918 completed by Robert Duncan & Co for the Shipping Controller and placed under the management of Lang & Fulton Ltd. 1920 sold to D & T G Adams of Newcastle-on-Tyne, and renamed *Nillemede*.

Part Five
The Fleet of P MacCallum & Sons Ltd 1919–74

1. *Ardgarth* (1922–24)
   See ship list. Part Three, No. 7.
2. *Ardgour* (1922–24)
   See ship list. Part Three, No. 11.
3. *Ardgarvel* (1922–27)
   See ship list. Part Three, No. 14.
4. *Ardgryfe* (II) (1922–59)
   See ship list. Part Three, No. 26.
5. *Ardgarroch* (II) (1922–37)
   See ship list. Part Three, No. 27.
6. *Ardglass* (III) (1919–35)
   See ship list. Part Three, No. 28.
7. *Ardgantock* (II) (1919–55)
   See ship list. Part Three, No. 29.
8. *Ardglen* (1953–72)
   1,044 gross tons, 507 net tons
   289 × 42 × 17 feet
   Two single acting 6 cylinder oil engines built by British Polar Engines Ltd, Glasgow
   1953 completed by James Lamont & Co, Port Glasgow for P MacCallum & Sons Ltd. Sold 1972 to Hortiatis Shipping Co. of Famagusta, renamed *Neni*.
9. *Ardgarry* (II) (1957–62)
   1,074 gross tons, 507 net tons
   221 × 34 × 13 feet
   Two single acting 6 cylinder oil engines built by British Polar Engines Ltd, Glasgow
   May 1957 completed by James Lamont & Co, Port Glasgow for P MacCallum & Sons Ltd. 1962 lost with all hands on passage from Swansea to Rouen with a cargo of coal.
10. *Ardgarvel* (II) (1965–74)
    1,121 gross tons, 486 net tons
    223 × 35 × 14 feet
    Two single acting 4 cylinder oil engines built by British Polar Engines Ltd, Glasgow
    September 1964 completed by James Lamont & Co, Port Glasgow for P MacCallum & Sons Ltd. Sold on 28 November 1974 to Henry W Peabody Grain Ltd, and renamed *Balmerino*. Acquired 1977 by Marpro Ltd, becoming their *Marigos Hope*, registered in London. Still on the 1979–80 register.

Part Six
Steamships managed for the Ministry of War Transport by P MacCallum & Sons Ltd
1941–47

1. *Margo* (1941–47)
   1,412 net tons
   321 × 34 × 14 feet
   Triple expansion 3 cylinder engines built by Flensburger Schiffsb Ges, Flensburg, Germany
   1895 completed by Flensburger Schiffsb Ges, Flensburg, Germany, for Dampschiff Rhederei van 1889, Hamburg, as *Gutrune*. 1902 sold to Woermann Linnie Kommandit Ges, and renamed *Linda Woermann*. 1916 requisitioned by the Portuguese Government and renamed *Pungue*. 1924 sold to S Denoliel & Sons, Lisbon, and renamed *Luna*. 1924 sold to Societe Anon Co-operative de Marseilles and renamed *Ville D'Alexandrette*. 1928 sold to Slobodna Plovidta Bokeska, Tivat, and renamed *Anton Iovic*. 1934 sold to Alfred Kahn and renamed *Margo*. 1941 requisitioned by Ministry of War Shipping and placed in the management of P MacCallum & Sons Ltd. First entry in MacCallums' Abstract Log Book 20 February 1941. 1947 condemned and scuttled.

2. *Empire Bank* (1941–42)
   402 net tons
   1941 completed by Henry Scarr Ltd of Hessle, Yorkshire, for Ministry of War Transport and placed in the management of Peter MacCallum & Sons. First entry in Abstract Log Book 4 August 1941, when vessel was at Hull. November 1942 transferred to management of Metcalf Motor Coasters Ltd. Taken over by Metcalfs in 1946, becoming their *Rose-Julie M*. In 1965 she was owned by the Mac Shipping Co, but she was not registered after 1946.

3. *Nordost* (about 1942–43)
   1,035 net tons
   215 × 34 × 15 feet
   Triple expansion 3 cylinder engines built by C A Kuijpers, Rotterdam
   1918 completed by De Haan & Oerlemans, Heusder as *Lifland*. 1940s owned by Reidera A/B Nord & Ostersjofort.

4. *Ophir* (about 1942–3)
   469 net tons
   155 × 26 × 10 feet
   Triple expansion 2 cylinder engines built by Ross & Duncan, Glasgow
   1907 completed by Ailsa Shipbuilding Co, Ayr, for Zillah Shipping & Carrying Co (W A Savage Ltd, managers), London. Owned by them until after the Second World War.

Part Seven
Vessel owned by Kindiesel Shipping Co

1. *Kindiesel* (1936–42)
   389 gross tons, 180 net tons
   136 × 25 × 9 feet
   Oil engines 2 cylinder by John G Kincaid & Co, Greenock
   1936 completed by Ardrossan Dry Dock & Shipbuilding Co for Kindiesel Shipping Co, managers P MacCallum & Sons. 1942 sold to Lovering & Sons, Cardiff.

Part Eight
Vessels managed for the Ministry of War Transport by the Kindiesel Shipping Co Ltd
1943–45

1. *Strait Fisher* (1943–44)
   573 gross tons
   104 × 27 × 11 feet
   Triple expansion 3 cylinder engines by J Lewis & Sons Ltd, Aberdeen
   1917 completed by J Lewis & Sons, Aberdeen. Owned by James Fisher & Sons Ltd, Barrow. Transferred to the Kindiesel Company in 1943, but out of their control by the end of 1944. Capsized and sank in 1945.

2. *Ann M* (1943–44)

   169 gross tons

   92 × 21 × 8 feet

   Oil engines 5 cylinder by L Gardner & Sons Ltd, Manchester

   1926 completed by J Pollock Sons & Co, Faversham as MV *Lido*. Acquired 1940 by Metcalf Motor Coasters Ltd, London, renamed *Ann M*. Transferred to the Kindiesel Company in 1943, out of their control by the end of 1944. Returned to Metcalfs and operated by them until 1962, when she was replaced by a vessel of the same name, built by the Burntisland Shipbuilding Co Ltd.

3. *David M* (1943–44)

   350 gross tons

   130 × 25 × 9 feet

   Oil engines 4 cylinder by Humbolds Deutz Motoren AG, Köln-Deutz

   1933 completed by J Koster, Groningen, Holland for Metcalf Motor Coasters Ltd (T J Metcalf, managers), London. Transferred to the Kindiesel Company in 1943, out of their control by the end of 1944. Returned to Metcalfs and operated by them, latterly as managers for the Wimaisa Shipping Co, until 1971, when replaced by a second-hand Dutch-built ship, the *Rottum* of 1957.

4. *Ngakoa* (1943–44)

   494 gross tons

   166 × 27 × 8 feet

   Oil engines 6 cylinder by M T M Werke Manheim AG, replaced 1963 with 8 cylinder Lister Blackstone engines

   1938 completed by de Groot & van Vliet, Slitkkerveer. Transferred to the Kindiesel Company in 1943, out of their control by end of 1944. Acquired by Metcalf Motor Coasters Ltd, and renamed *Thomas M.* in 1946. Acquired 1967 by Zoulias Bros, Piraeus, becoming their *Milos III*. Sold 1973 to Lynbrook Maritime SA, when her name was changed to *Maria S*. She became the *Maria Cia* in the following year, and was sold in 1976 to Ourania Xafas and K Tseleritis, Piraeus, who renamed her *Evangelia*. Still on the register in 1979–80.

5. *Nordost* (1943–45)

   Transferred from MacCallums (see part 6 of ship list)

   Last entry in Abstract Log Book 27 August 1945

6. *Margo* (1943–45)

   Transferred from MacCallums (see part 6 of ship list)

   Last entry in Abstract Log Book 1 March 1945.

7. *Ophir* (1943–45)

   Transferred from MacCallums (see part 6 of ship list)

   Last entry in Abstract Log Book 16 October 1945.

142

List of Directors of P MacCallum & Sons Ltd, 1907–1982

Peter MacCallum Lang	1907–1930	
Louis Vandalle Fulton	1907–1934	
John Dunlop Dempster	1909–1918;	1920–
	1950	
James Fulton, junior	1918–1924	
John James Lang	1918–1937	
Charles MacKinlay Duncan	1919–1937	
Charles Gibson Fulton	1924–1936	
Ian MacCallum Lang	1932–1980	
James Vandalle Fulton	1934–1945	
Robert Waterston Fulton	1938–1944	
John Burton Lang	1938–1941;	1951–
	1975	
Hugh Crawford Waterston	1939–1961	
Thomas D R Taylor	1957–1961	
Robert I Clark	1961–1969	
James Fulton Lang	1962–	
Walter P. McLean	1963–1971	
Peter MacCallum Lang	1967–	
Robin L V Fulton	1971–	
John Macdonald	1971–	
Ian Bruce Lang	1976–1981	

Index

Where a page number is italicized, this indicates that the reference is to be found in an illustration or table

144

Dr   Peter

Date (1862)	No.		Account	£	s	d	
May 29	258	To	Bills Payable	2041	16	3	✓
June 25	265	"	Cash	1800	"	"	✓
" 12	267	"	Bills Payable	1498	5	8	✓
"	268	"	Discount	56	5	4	✓
July 25	273	"	Cash	1500	"	"	✓
" 9	274	"	Bills Payable	800	3	6	✓
Sept 4	284	"	Cash	2300	"	"	✓
" 15	286	"	Bills Payable	2000	"	"	✓
" 4	287	"	Discount	95	"	"	✓
Oct 8	292	"	Cash	500	"	"	✓
" "	293	"	Bills Payable	1200	"	"	✓
" 14	293	"	do	1274	14	2	
" 8	294	"	Discount	12	10	"	
Nov 21	300	"	Bills Payable	2450	"	"	
Dec 24	308	"	do	2484	16	2	
Feby 5	322	"	do	1118	15	4	
March 3	330	"	do	1749	18	4	
April 9	339	"	do	1267	17	4	
May 12	345	"	do	"	12	8	
" 9	347	"	Bills Payable	750	"	"	
June 5	355	"	do	684	13	"	
" 27	356	"	do	853	1	10	
" 3	357	"	Building Yard	106	"	"	
							28574	8	10
1863							
July 28	365	To	Bills Payable	962	5	4	
							962	5	4
1863							
Sept 9	380	To	Bills Payable	812	4	"	
" 25	381	"		791	16	2	
							1604	"	2
1863							
" 9	400	To	Bills Payable	253	8	11	
							253	8	11
1864							
Feby 9	421	To	Bills Payable	1043	3	4	
" "	422	"	do	900	1	4	
							1943	4	8